A GLOSSARY OF LITERARY TERMS

A GLOSSARY OF LITERARY TERMS

By M. H. Abrams, *Cornell University*

BASED ON THE ORIGINAL VERSION BY

Dan S. Norton and Peters Rushton

HOLT, RINEHART AND WINSTON   New York

FOREWORD

As a teacher whose work has for years been facilitated by Norton and Rushton's engaging *Glossary*, I welcomed the invitation to revise this useful little book and bring it up to date. It quickly became evident, however, that patchwork emendation would produce a hybrid something that would have pleased the late authors no more than it did the editor. I have therefore rewritten the text in its entirety and have also added well over one hundred terms to the original version. The additions include a number of useful older terms—*abstract and concrete, criticism, diction, folio, humanism, primitivism, style,* and many others—together with such more recent commonplaces as *ambiguity, archetype, emotive language, the new criticism, empathy, tension,* and (the choice was inevitable) *objective correlative.* The aim throughout has been to supplement the preferred definition of a term with enough indications of its semantic changes in time, and of its diversity in present usage, to provide the student with a chart by which to steer a course through the shifting referents and submerged ambiguities of literary discussion.

For introductory courses in literature, and for courses in literary history and criticism, I have found it a great convenience to assign a selected set of terms from the *Glossary* week by week as these become pertinent to the materials under consideration. In this way the lecturer avoids breaking the continuity of his discussion to interject definitions that can be studied more conveniently and accurately at the student's leisure, and from a printed text. The present *Glossary* has been designed to be useful also in advanced courses and as a handy reference book for the general reader. The range of the topics, both critical and historical, is wide; the analyses lend themselves to refinement and expansion in class; and the references to sources, examples, and authoritative larger treatments invite the reader to go on to explore the more important subjects on his own.

The entries have been organized as a series of essays, alphabetically arranged, in which minor terms are usually discussed under the major or generic terms to which they are related. To lighten the cross-indexing, separate alphabetical entries have been omitted for compound terms which include the class name under which they are discussed. Thus, *comedy of manners* and *high comedy* will be found under *Comedy, practical criticism* under *Criticism, dramatic irony* under *Irony,* and *slant rhyme* under *Rhyme.*

This *Glossary* has profited greatly from the learning and acumen of my colleague, Professor W. R. Keast.

M. H. A.

January, 1957

Abstract and Concrete. A sentence is sometimes said to be abstract if it makes a general statement about a class of things or persons ("All men are created equal") as opposed to a particular statement about an individual object or person ("Grishkin is nice . . ."). More commonly it is said to be abstract if its subject is an "abstraction"; that is, if it is the name for a quality—"beauty," "brightness," "heat"—which cannot exist apart from the object or situation of which it is an attribute, or if it is the name for an entity—"poetry," "reason," "force"—which cannot be perceived by the senses. Shakespeare's "Ripeness is all" and Pope's

> Hope springs eternal in the human breast,
> Man never is, but always to be, blest,

are both abstract. "Concrete" is the term applied to a sentence which refers to particular, perceivable things and situations. When Dante said of God,

> His will is our peace,

he made a statement involving the abstractions "will" and "peace." In the line immediately following,

> It is that sea to which all moves,

Dante supplemented the abstract statement with the more concrete instance of the eternal movement of all waters to their abiding place, the sea. Usually, however, critics reserve the word "concrete" for statements which are not only about particular and perceivable things, but also present their sensuous qualities with uncommon vividness and detail. A familiar example is Keats's

> And still she slept an azure-lidded sleep,
> In blanchèd linen, smooth, and lavendered,
> While he from forth the closet brought a heap
> Of candied apple, quince, and plum, and gourd;
> With jellies soother than the creamy curd,
> And lucent syrops, tinct with cinnamon.

Accent. See **Meter.**

Act. A major division of the action of a play. The division into acts was brought into English drama by the Elizabethan writers (see **Elizabethan Age**), who followed their Roman models by writing plays in five acts. Modern plays are commonly divided into three acts.

Acts are subdivided into scenes, each of which consists of a unit of action in which there is no change of place or break in the continuity of time. Nowadays the end of a scene is usually indicated by dropping the curtain.

Aesthetic distance. See **Objective and Subjective.**

Affective fallacy. See **Criticism.**

Alexandrine. See **Meter.**

Allegory. An allegory undertakes to make a doctrine or thesis interesting and persuasive by converting it into a narrative in which the agents, and sometimes the setting as well, represent general concepts, moral qualities, or other abstractions. In *The Pilgrim's Progress* Bunyan allegorizes his doctrine of Christian salvation by telling how Christian, warned by Evangelist, flees from the City of Destruction and makes his way toilsomely to the Celestial City; en route he encounters such characters as Faithful, Hopeful, and the Giant Despair, and wins through places like the Slough of Despond, the Valley of the Shadow of Death, and Vanity Fair. A paragraph from this work will give a glimpse of the allegorical process:

> Now as Christian was walking solitary by himself, he espied one afar off come crossing over the field to meet him; and their hap was to meet just as they were crossing the way of each other. The Gentleman's name was Mr. Worldly-Wiseman; he dwelt in the Town of Carnal-Policy, a very great Town, and also hard by from whence Christian came.

A great variety of literary forms have been used for allegory. The medieval *Everyman* is an allegorical drama, Spenser's *Faerie Queene* an allegorical romance, *The Pilgrim's Progress* an allegorical prose narrative, and William Collins' *Ode on the Poetical Character* an allegorical lyric poem. See **Didactic, personification** (under **Figurative language**), **Plot and Character;** and consult C. S. Lewis, *The Allegory of Love* (1936).

A **fable** is a story, exemplifying a moral thesis, in which animals talk and act like human beings. In the fable of the fox and the grapes, the fox, after unsuccessfully exerting all his wiles to get the grapes hanging beyond his reach, concludes that they are probably sour anyway. The moral is that we tend to belittle what we can't have ourselves. The most famous collection of fables is attributed to the Greek writer, Aesop; another notable collection was written by La Fontaine, a Frenchman of the seventeenth century. John Gay and many other English authors wrote fables, and so did the American writers Joel Chandler Harris, in his Uncle Remus stories, and James Thurber, in his *Fables for Our Time.*

A **parable** also enforces a moral or other kind of doctrine, but not, like allegory, by the actions of abstract personifications, nor, like fable, by a narrative in which animals are the agents. Instead, a parable is a short narrative, presented so as to bring out the analogy, or parallel, between its elements and a lesson that the speaker is trying to bring home to us. The parable was one of Christ's favorite literary devices; examples are His parables of the sower, of the Good Samaritan, and of the wise and foolish virgins. Here is the short parable of the fruit trees that Christ used in instructing His listeners how to detect false prophets (Matthew 7:16–20):

> Ye shall know them by their fruits. Do men gather grapes of thorns, or figs of thistles? Even so every good tree bringeth forth good fruit; but a corrupt tree bringeth forth evil fruit. A good tree cannot bring forth evil fruit, neither can a corrupt tree bring forth good fruit. Every tree that bringeth not forth good fruit is hewn down, and cast into the fire. Wherefore by their fruits ye shall know them.

An **exemplum** was a story told by medieval preachers as a particular instance illustrating the general text of a sermon; the story was usually claimed to be true. In Chaucer's *Pardoner's Tale*, the Pardoner, preaching on the text, "Greed is the root of all evil," presents by way of exemplum the story of the three revelers who set out to find Death, but find a heap of gold instead, then kill one another in the attempt to gain sole possession of the treasure. Chaucer's Chanticleer borrows the preacher's technique in the ten exempla he tells in a vain effort to persuade his sceptical wife, Dame Pertelote the hen, that bad dreams forbode disaster.

Alliteration is the repetition of consonants, especially at the beginning of words or of stressed syllables. In Old English poetry alliteration was a regular element of each line, but since then it has been used for special effects only:

> The *b*lazing *b*rightness of her *b*eauties *b*eame,
> And glorious light of her *s*unshiny face
> To tell, were as to *s*trive against the *s*treame.
> SPENSER

Consonance is the repetition of a pattern of consonants, with changes in the intervening vowels: live-love, hill-hall, lean-alone. W. H. Auden's " 'O where are you going?' said reader to rider," makes prominent use of this device; the last stanza reads:

> "Out of this house"—said *rider* to *reader*,
> "Yours never will"—said *farer* to *fearer*,
> "They're looking for you"—said *hearer* to *horror*,
> As he left them there, as he left them there.[1]

Assonance is the repetition of identical or related vowel sounds, especially in stressed syllables. Note the recurrent *a* and *u* sounds in Coleridge's

> In X*a*n*a*d*u* did K*u*bl*a* Kh*a*n
> A st*a*tely ple*a*s*u*re dome decree.

[1] From Song XXV in *The Collected Poetry of W. H. Auden,* copyright 1945 by W. H. Auden.

Rhyme can be regarded as a special instance of both vowel and consonant repetition; see **Rhyme**. For other sound effects in verse, see **Euphony and Cacophony** and **Onomatopeia**.

Allusion in poetry is a brief reference to a person, place, or event assumed to be sufficiently well known to be recognized by the reader. In Thomas Nashe's

> Brightness falls from the air,
> Queens have died young and fair,
> Dust hath closed Helen's eye;
> I am sick, I must die.
> Lord, have mercy on us!

the allusion is to Helen of Troy. Gray's lines about Eton,

> Ye distant spires, ye antique towers,
> That crown the watery glade,
> Where grateful Science still adores
> Her Henry's Holy Shade,

contain an allusion to Henry VI, the founder of Eton College.

Ambiguity. Since William Empson published *Seven Types of Ambiguity* (1930), this term has been widely used to signify that often, in poetry, two or more meanings of a word or phrase are relevant. "Multiple meaning" and "plurisignation" are alternate terms for the same phenomenon; they have the advantage of avoiding the implication, in the ordinary use of "ambiguity," that the quality is a stylistic fault rather than a valuable poetic device.

When Shakespeare's Cleopatra, exciting the asp to a frenzy, says,

> Come, thou mortal wretch,
> With thy sharp teeth this knot intrinsicate
> Of life at once untie; poor venemous fool,
> Be angry, and despatch—,

her speech is richly multiple in significance. For example, "mortal" means "fatal" or "death-dealing," and at the same time serves as a reminder that the asp is itself mortal, or subject to death. "Wretch" is a contemptuous epithet, yet also expresses pity (Cleopatra goes on to refer to the asp as "my baby at my breast, That sucks the nurse asleep"). And the two meanings of "despatch"—"make haste" and "kill"—are equally relevant. Compare **Connotation and Denotation** and **pun** (under **Figurative language**).

"Intrinsicate" in the same passage exemplifies a special type of multiple meaning, the **portmanteau word**. The term was introduced into literary criticism by Humpty Dumpty, in explicating to Alice the meaning of the opening lines of "Jabberwocky":

'Twas brillig, and the slithy toves
Did gyre and gimble in the wabe.

"Slithy," Humpty Dumpty explained, "means 'lithe and slimy'. . . . You see it's like a portmanteau—there are two meanings packed up into one word." A portmanteau word, then, is a word coined by fusing two other words; thus Shakespeare's "intrinsicate" is a blend of "intrinsic" and "intricate." James Joyce exploited this device to the full in order to sustain the multiple levels of meaning in his dream narrative, *Finnegans Wake.*

Anapest. See **Meter.**

Anecdote. See **Short story.**

Annal. See **Chronicle.**

Antagonist. See **Plot and Character.**

Anticlimax. See **Pathos and Bathos.**

Antistrophe. See **Ode.**

Antithesis. See **Couplet.**

Apostrophe. See **Rhetorical figures.**

Archaism. See **Diction.**

Archetype is a term much used since the 1930's, when it was imported into criticism from the depth psychology of C. G. Jung. Jung described archetypes as "primordial images" formed by repeated experiences in the lives of our ancestors, inherited in the "collective unconscious" of the human race, and often expressed in myths, religion, dreams, and fantasies, as well as in literature. In literary criticism the term "archetype" (or "archetypal image" or "archetypal pattern") is applied to a character type or plot pattern or description which recurs frequently in literature and folklore and is thought to evoke profound emotional responses in the reader because it resonates with an image already existing in his unconscious mind. The death-rebirth theme is often said to be the basic archetype. Some other patterns frequently traced in literature are the journey under the sea, the Paradise-Hades archetype, and the archetypal images of the Fatal Woman, the ruthless Male Hero, the Devil, and God. An influential book on the subject is Maud Bodkin's *Archetypal Patterns in Poetry* (1934). Compare **Stock characters.**

Article. See **Essay.**

Assonance. See **Alliteration.**

Atmosphere is the mood pervading a literary work, setting up in the reader expectations as to the course of events, whether happy or (more commonly) disastrous. Shakespeare establishes the tense and fearful atmosphere of *Hamlet* by the terse and nervous dialogue of the opening; Coleridge engenders a strange compound of religious and superstitious terror by his manner of describing the initial scene of "Christabel"; and Hardy, in *The Return of the Native,* makes Egdon Heath an immense and brooding presence which reduces to pettiness and futility the human struggle for happiness for which it is the setting. See **Setting.**

Augustan Age. In its original application, the Augustan Age was the brilliant literary age of Virgil, Horace, and Ovid under the Roman emperor Augustus (27 B.C.–A.D. 14). Oliver Goldsmith and other eighteenth-century writers applied the name by analogy to England during the reign of Queen Anne (1702–1714). The term is now most frequently applied to the first forty-five years of the eighteenth century, the age of Pope, Swift, Addison, and Steele, although occasionally (as in George Saintsbury's *The Peace of the Augustans*) the term is used to cover the whole eighteenth century. See **Neoclassic and Romantic** and, for some prominent literary forms in this period, **Couplet, Satire, Sensibility and Sentimentalism.**

Autobiography. See **Biography.**

Ballad. A convenient thumbnail definition of the ballad is that it is a song—usually a short song—that tells a story. The **folk ballad** or **popular ballad** is one whose author (if it had a single author) is unknown, and which has been transmitted from singer to singer by word of mouth. Since the individual singer is apt to introduce changes in both words and tune, the ballad can be said to be recomposed each time it is rendered. Typically, the folk ballad is impersonal and dramatic; it centers on the climactic episode in the story, tells it tersely through dialogue and action without comment by the author, and explains what has gone before, if at all, chiefly by brief allusion in the dialogue. The most common stanza form—called the **ballad stanza**—is a quatrain in alternate 4- and 3-stress lines, rhyming abcb. This is the form of "Sir Patrick Spens"; the first stanza of this ballad also exemplifies the conventionally abrupt opening and the manner of proceeding by briefly described action and curt dialogue:

> The king sits in Dumferling towne
> Drinking the blude-red wine:
> "O whar will I get a guid sailor,
> To sail this schip of mine?"

The ballad frequently uses set formulas, among them: (1) the refrain ("Edward," "Lord Randall"), (2) stock descriptive phrases like "milk-white steed" and "blood-red wine," and (3) **incremental repetition,** or the repetition of a preceding stanza with a variation that advances the narrative ("Lord Randall," "Child Waters"). See **refrain** under **Stanza.**

The standard collection of folk ballads is Francis J. Child's *English and Scottish Popular Ballads* (1882–1898), also available in an abridged version edited by H. C. Sargent and G. L. Kittredge (1904). It must be remembered, however, that a published version gives only one of many variant forms of a ballad and presents only the verbal skeleton, without the song. Ballads are still being sung—and collected—in the British Isles and in the rural areas of America, especially along the Atlantic seaboard and in the adjoining hill country. For a study of the folk ballad, see G. H. Gerould, *The Ballad of Tradition* (1932).

The **literary ballad** is one written in deliberate imitation of the form and spirit of a folk ballad. Some of the most successful were written in the Romantic period: Coleridge's "Rime of the Ancient Mariner" (which is, however, much longer and more elaborate than the folk ballad), Scott's "Proud Maisie," and Keats's "La Belle Dame sans Merci."

Bathos. See **Pathos and Bathos.**

Biography. Late in the seventeenth century, Dryden defined biography as "the history of particular men's lives." The name now connotes a relatively full account of the facts of a man's life, involving the attempt, by description and analysis, to recreate his character, personality, and milieu. That the writing of biography is a literary art is indicated by the slow development of its methods and devices since Plutarch's *Parallel Lives* of Greek and Roman notables, written early in the second century A.D. English biography proper, as distinguished from the commemorative and didactic saints' lives of the Middle Ages, appeared in the sixteenth century. By the eighteenth century both the theory and practice of biography had greatly advanced; that age produced Dr. Johnson's monumental *Lives of the English Poets* and James Boswell's *Life of Samuel Johnson,* which many hold to be the greatest biography ever written. Two especially notable biographies of men of letters written in the nineteenth century were John Lockhart's *Life of Scott* and John Forster's *Life of Charles Dickens.* In our own time biography has become a very popular literary form, and one or another biographical title usually stands high on the best-seller list. See Harold Nicolson, *The Development of English Biography* (1928) and two works by Donald A. Stauffer, *English Biography before 1700* (1930), and *The Art of Biography in Eighteenth Century England* (1941).

Autobiography is a biography written by the subject himself. It should be distinguished from private diaries and journals, which are day-to-day accounts of the events in a man's life kept for his own use and pleasure; examples of such writings, which were not intended for publication, are the *Diaries* of Samuel Pepys and John Evelyn, and the *Journals* of James Boswell. One of the greatest of autobiographies, the *Confessions* of St. Augustine, was written as early as the fourth century A.D. Some of the better-known English and American autobiographies are those by John Stuart Mill, Anthony Trollope, Benjamin Franklin, and Henry Adams.

Blank verse is unrhymed iambic pentameter verse (see **Meter**). Of all the regular English verse forms it is the most fluid and comes closest to the natural rhythms of English speech, yet it is readily heightened for passages of passion and grandeur. Soon after blank verse was introduced by Surrey in the sixteenth century, it was adopted as the standard meter for Elizabethan drama; a free form of blank verse is still found in modern poetic dramas such as those by Maxwell Anderson and T. S. Eliot. Milton used blank verse for the epic, *Paradise Lost,* James Thomson for his descriptive and philosophical *Seasons,* Wordsworth for his autobiographical *Prelude,* Tennyson for the narrative *Idylls of the King,* and Browning for many of his dramatic monologues. A number of long meditative lyrics have also been written in blank verse, among which are Coleridge's "Frost at Midnight" and Wordsworth's "Tintern Abbey." Blank verse lacks the rhyme which usually sets the pattern for stanza divisions (see **Stanza**), but some poets write blank verse so that it falls into rhetorical units called **verse paragraphs;** these units can readily be detected in Milton's *Paradise Lost* and Wordsworth's *Prelude.* The beginning and end of the opening verse paragraph from Wordsworth's "Tintern Abbey" will show the music and flexibility of which blank verse is capable in the hands of a master. Notice the shifts in stress, managed so that they give the effect of a living voice without violating the basic iambic pulse; the way the end of a syntactical unit sometimes coincides with the end of a line and sometimes runs on beyond it; the variation of the caesural pauses within the lines; and the ever-renewing run of the lyric voice up to the cadence that concludes the paragraph:

> Five years have past; five summers, with the length
> Of five long winters! And again I hear
> These waters, rolling from their mountain-springs
> With a soft inland murmur.—Once again
> Do I behold these steep and lofty cliffs,
> That on a wild secluded scene impress
> Thoughts of more deep seclusion; and connect
> The landscape with the quiet of the sky.
> 　　　　　　　. . . Once again I see
> These hedge-rows, hardly hedge-rows, little lines
> Of sportive wood run wild: these pastoral farms,
> Green to the very door; and wreaths of smoke

> Sent up, in silence, from among the trees!
> With some uncertain notice, as might seem,
> Of vagrant dwellers in the houseless woods,
> Or of some Hermit's cave, where by his fire
> The Hermit sits alone.

Bombast originally meant "cotton stuffing," and the word was adopted to describe verbose and pretentious diction, inflated out of proportion to the meaning and situation. In Christopher Marlowe's *Dr. Faustus,* Faustus says:

> Now by the kingdoms of infernal rule,
> Of Styx, Acheron, and the fiery lake
> Of ever-burning Phlegethon, I swear
> That I do long to see the monuments
> And situation of bright-splendent Rome;

which is no more than to say: "By Hades, I'd like to see Rome!" Marlowe's attempt to heighten the flat, literal statement, so successful elsewhere in the play, is here ludicrously inappropriate to the occasion. (See **Diction.**) Bombast is the staple of the conversation of Shakespeare's comic character Pistol, in *Henry IV, Part 2,* and *Henry V.* An amusing parody of the frequent bombast in the heroic drama of the late seventeenth and early eighteenth centuries is Henry Fielding's play, *Tom Thumb,* written in 1730 (see **heroic drama** under **Tragedy**).

Bourgeois tragedy. See **Tragedy.**

Bowdlerize. To bowdlerize is to expurgate the parts of a work considered indecent or indelicate. The word derives from Thomas Bowdler, who tidied up his *Family Shakespeare* in 1818 by omitting "whatever is unfit to be read by a gentleman in the company of ladies." *Gulliver's Travels,* Shakespeare, and the Bible are frequently bowdlerized in editions intended for children, and even some compilers of college anthologies avail themselves of Bowdler's prerogative in editing the text of Chaucer.

Bucolic poetry. See **Pastoral.**

Burlesque and Parody. "Burlesque," "parody," "caricature," and "travesty" are often used interchangeably, but to equate the terms in this way is to surrender very useful critical distinctions. It is better to use **burlesque** as the generic term for all literary forms in which people, actions, or other literary works are made ridiculous by an incongruous imitation, and to reserve the other terms as names for various species of burlesque. When the laugh is raised (as it usually is), not for its own sake, but to deride some person or object existing outside the burlesque itself, burlesque in its various species serves as a vehicle of satire (see **Satire**). It should be added that an extended work of burlesque is usually flexible enough to exploit a variety of the devices listed below. We name it by the device that it uses most persistently; accordingly, we say that Pope's *Rape of the Lock* is a mock epic, although it includes many more than specifically mock-epic devices.

When the incongruity arises from treating a trivial subject in an elevated and serious manner, we get "high burlesque"; when it arises from treating a serious subject in a low and comic manner, we get "low burlesque." A **mock epic** (see under **Epic**) employs the conventional attributes and the elaborate style of the epic genre to make a trivial and commonplace subject laughable. A **parody,** like the mock epic, is also a form of high burlesque, but it derides, not its subject, but a particular literary work or style, by imitating its features and applying them to trivial or grossly discordant materials. John Phillips' "The Splendid Shilling" (1705) was an early parody of the style of Milton's *Paradise Lost,* applied to the subject of a starveling writer composing in a garret. Henry Fielding parodied Richardson's *Pamela,* first in *Shamela* and later in *Joseph Andrews.* Compare the first stanza of Wordsworth's "She Dwelt among the Untrodden Ways" with the first stanza of Hartley Coleridge's parody:

> He lived amidst th' untrodden ways
> To Rydal Lake that lead;
> A bard whom there were none to praise,
> And very few to read.

One type of low burlesque is the **Hudibrastic,** named from Samuel Butler's *Hudibras* (1663), which describes the ridiculous adventures of a Puritan knight, not in the high style appropriate to the romance of knighthood, but in a jingly meter and ludicrously colloquial idiom. Another, the **travesty,** mocks a specific work by treating its lofty subject in grotesquely extravagant or lowly terms; as Boileau put it, in a travesty of the *Aeneid* "Dido and Aeneas are made to speak like fishwives and ruffians."

Caricature is a type of portrait which makes a person ludicrous by exaggerating or distorting prominent features without losing the likeness. The term is commonly applied to drawings or paintings, but literature has its analogues in the quick verbal sketch of the quintessential appearance. Pope in *The Rape of the Lock* described Sir Plume, "With earnest eyes, and round unthinking face," and Burns caricatured the strait-laced prudes of his day as they sat at a revival meeting "Wi' screw'd up, grace-proud faces." A **lampoon** is a full-length verbal portrait of an individual in which he is ridiculed in a biting and often scurrilous manner. Pope's satiric portrait of "Atticus" (Addison) in his "Epistle to Dr. Arbuthnot" transforms the individual too completely into a permanent type—the genius lamed by a malice that is rendered impotent by timidity—to be properly called a lampoon; his caustic portrayal of Colley Cibber in *The Dunciad,* however, constitutes an indubitable lampoon.

See **Satire** and **Wit and Humor,** and refer to Richmond P. Bond, *English Burlesque Poetry* (1932), and Walter Jerrold and R. M. Leonard, editors, *A Century of Parody and Imitation* (1913).

Cacophony. See **Euphony.**

Caesura. See **Meter.**

Caricature. See **Burlesque and Parody.**

Caroline Period is the name for the reign of Charles I, 1625–1649, in which was fought the English Civil War. During this period Milton began to write; it was also the age of the **Cavalier Poets** (Robert Herrick, Thomas Carew, Sir John Suckling, and Richard Lovelace), of the religious poet George Herbert, and of the prose writers Robert Burton and Sir Thomas Browne.

Carpe diem. See **Motif.**

Catastrophe. See **Plot and Character.**

Catharsis. See **Tragedy.**

Cavalier Poets. See **Caroline Period.**

Character. For "the character" as a literary form, see **Novel;** for "character" as a person in a story, see **Plot and Character.**

Chiasmus. See **Rhetorical figures.**

Chorus. In early Greek times the chorus was a band of men who performed songs and dances at religious festivals. Gradually speaking parts were added, until from this choral celebration developed Greek drama. In the early Greek tragedies the songs of the chorus made up the greater part of the play, but later the chorus became a group of onlookers who commented intermittently on the action without affecting its evolution. See **Comedy** and **Tragedy.**

The Roman playwrights took the chorus from the Greeks, and in the middle of the sixteenth century some English dramatists (e.g., Norton and Sackville in *Gorboduc*) imitated the use of the chorus by the Romans. The classical chorus, however, was never widely used by English writers; the only literary masterpiece which includes this feature is John Milton's tragedy, *Samson Agonistes*. During the Elizabethan Age the term "chorus" was sometimes applied to a single character who spoke the prologue and epilogue to a play, as in Marlowe's *Dr. Faustus* and Shakespeare's *King Henry V*. Modern scholars sometimes use the term **choral character** to identify a person in a play, such as the Fool in *King Lear* or Enobarbus in *Antony and Cleopatra*, who stands somewhat apart from the action and by his comments provides the audience with a perspective through which to view characters and events. A character with a somewhat similar function is the **confidant** (feminine, **confidante**), who has little effect on the action but serves the protagonist as a trusted friend to whom he can confess his intimate thoughts. The confidant thus provides the author of a play or novel with a plausible device for revealing the mind and intentions of a principal character. Horatio is Hamlet's confidant, and Maria Gostrey is the confidante of Strether in Henry James's *The Ambassadors*.

Chronicle. Chronicles, the predecessors of modern "histories," were extended accounts, in either verse or prose, of national or world-wide events over a considerable period of time. Unlike the modern historian, however, the chronicler took his information where he found it and made little attempt to separate fact from legend. **Annals** differ from chronicles in being summary notices of the events taking place in a single locale or nation, recorded year by year. The most notable English chronicles are the *Anglo-Saxon Chronicles*, started by King Alfred in the ninth century and continued until the twelfth century, and the Elizabethan *Chronicles* of England, Ireland, and Scotland by Raphael Holinshed and other writers (1577).

Chronicle plays are dramatic renderings of materials taken from the chronicle histories of England (see **Chronicle**). They came into sudden popularity in the last decade of the sixteenth century, when the fervor of patriotism following the defeat of the Spanish Armada brought a demand for plays dealing with the events of English history. At first chronicle plays presented a loosely knit series of events that occurred during the reign of an English king, and they depended for their effects mainly on a great bustle of stage battles, pageantry, and spectacle. Marlowe, however, in his *Edward II*, selected and rearranged the material in Holinshed's *Chronicles* to compose a unified drama of character; and Shakespeare's series of chronicle plays, encompassing the succession of English kings from Richard II to Henry VIII, includes such masterpieces as *Richard II* and *Henry IV, Parts 1 and 2*. See Felix E. Schelling, *The English Chronicle Play* (1902).

Cliché is French for the stereotype plate used in printing. Applied to diction, it signifies an expression which deviates enough from the ordinary or the literal usage to call attention to itself and which has been used so often that it is felt to be trite and tedious. "Point with pride," "nipped in the bud," "pole out a four-bagger," "my better half," "the home beautiful," are familiar examples of such hackneyed verbal formulas. The farther a phrase departs from ordinary usage, the more readily and conspicuously does it become a cliché.

> Come, and trip it as you go
> On the light fantastic toe,

was quaintly charming in Milton's "L'Allegro"; but "to trip the light fantastic" as a substitute for "to dance" is now an annoying instance of false elegance. Standard Fourth of July and Commencement oratory, the writings of many sports columnists, commercial greeting cards, and the slang of up-to-date teen-agers are rich mines of clichés. "Epiphany," "redemption," "levels of meaning," "dissociation of sensibility," have become clichés of contemporary literary criticism; and with some alteration, Pope's satiric comment on the clichés of eighteenth-century versifiers would apply to Tin Pan Alley, as it did to Grub Street:

> Where'er you find "the cooling western breeze,"
> In the next line it "whispers through the trees";
> If crystal streams "with pleasing murmurs creep,"
> The reader's threatened (not in vain) with "sleep."

See **stock response** under **Stock characters.**

Climax. See **Plot and Character.**

Comedy. The term "comedy" is now broadly applied to works (especially in the dramatic form) in which the characters undergo embarrassments or discomfitures which are on the whole so managed that they interest and amuse us without engaging our profoundest sympathy, and in which the action turns out well for the chief characters. (Compare **Tragedy.**) English comedy developed in the sixteenth century from such native materials as the farcical episodes introduced in the medieval drama (see **Miracle and Morality plays**), together with elements of character, action, and construction derived from the Roman comedy of Plautus and Terence. Nicholas Udall's *Ralph Roister Doister* (*ca.* 1533), the earliest known English comedy, exemplifies this combination. Comedy rapidly achieved a high stage of development in the Elizabethan Age. Shakespeare wrote various types, including the Roman form, such as *The Comedy of Errors* (based on a play by Plautus), and **romantic comedy** (*As You Like It, Twelfth Night*), in which the central situation is a love affair, involving a beautiful and idealized heroine, the course of which does not run smoothly but ends well. Ben Jonson's plays, such as *The Alchemist* and *Volpone,* are masterpieces of **satiric comedy,** which ridicule violations of moral and social standards by one or more rascally swindlers, as well as the greed and gullibility of their victims. (See **intrigue** under **Plot and Character**.) Restoration dramatists brought to the peak of its development the **comedy of manners;** this form deals with the relations and intrigues of gentlemen and ladies living in a polished and sophisticated society, evokes laughter mainly at the violations of social conventions and decorum, and relies for its effect in great part on the wit and sparkle of the dialogue (see **Wit and Humor**). Excellent examples are Congreve's *Way of the World* and Wycherley's *The Country Wife*. A reaction against the immorality of situation and the indecency of dialogue in **Restoration comedy** resulted in the **sentimental comedy** of the eighteenth century, dealing with monumentally noble heroes and heroines of the middle class who utter sentiments of unimpeachable rectitude and suffer tribulations which, incongruously, are managed so that they evoke tears, rather than smiles, from the audience (see **Sensibility and Sentimentalism**). Good examples of this type are Richard Steele's *The Conscious Lovers* and Richard Cumberland's *The West Indian*. Goldsmith and Sheridan, late in the century, revived the fun and wit, though not the indecency, of the Restoration comedy of manners. After a lapse in the earlier nineteenth century, good comedy was brought back to the stage by Oscar Wilde, A. W. Pinero, and others. Our own century, the age of J. M. Synge, George Bernard Shaw, Noel Coward, and many others, has been an eminent one for this dramatic form.

Some other distinctions are often made in discussing comedy. **High comedy** was a term introduced by George Meredith in *The Idea of Comedy* (1877) to define the comedy of manners that evokes "intellectual laughter"—laughter from spectators who remain emotionally detached from the action—at the spectacle of human folly and incongruity. A peak of high comedy is to be found in the wit combats of such intelligent, sophisticated, and well-matched lovers as Benedick and Beatrice in Shakespeare's *Much Ado about Nothing*, and Millamant and Mirabell in Congreve's *Way of the World.* **Low comedy,** on the other hand, makes no intellectual appeal, but depends for its comic effect on violent and boisterous action, or **slapstick:** the Mack Sennett films and the Chaplin one-reelers were unalloyed examples of this type. **Farce** often makes use of low-comedy episodes; it is a type of comedy in which one-dimensional characters are put into ludicrous situations, while ordinary standards of probability in motivation and event are freely violated in order to evoke the maximum laughter from an audience. Examples of excellent farce range from the horseplay of Shakespeare's *Taming of the Shrew* to the polished satire of Molière's *The Imaginary Invalid* and the verbal pyrotechnics of Wilde's *The Importance of Being Earnest*. For further discussions, see **Plot and Character, comic** (under **Satire**), and **Wit and Humor.**

Refer to A. H. Thorndike, *English Comedy* (1929) and Louis Kronenberger, *The Thread of Laughter* (1952).

Comedy of humors. See **Wit and Humor.**

Comic relief. See **Tragedy.**

Commonwealth Period, also known as the **Puritan Period,** extends from the end of the Civil War in 1649 to the Restoration in 1660. At this time England was ruled by Parliament under the control of the Puritan leader, Oliver Cromwell. Drama almost disappeared, because the Puritans closed the public theaters on moral and religious grounds. Milton wrote his prose political pamphlets at this time; it was the age of the prose writers Sir Thomas Browne, Thomas Fuller, and Izaak Walton, and of the poets Vaughan, Waller, Cowley, Davenant, and Marvell.

Conceit. Originally meaning simply an idea or image, "conceit" has come to be applied to a figure of speech which establishes a striking parallel—usually an elaborate parallel—between two apparently dissimilar things or situations (see **simile** and **metaphor** under **Figurative language**). The term was once derogatory, but it is now best employed as a neutral way of identifying a literary device. Two species of conceits are often distinguished. **Petrarchan conceits** are a type of figure used in love poems, which had been novel enough in their original employment by the Italian poet Petrarch but tended to become conventional and hackneyed in his imitators, the Elizabethan sonneteers. They consisted of elaborate and hyperbolical comparisons applied to the disdainful mistress, as cruel as she was beautiful, and to the distresses of the worshipful lover (see **hyperbole** under **Figurative language**). In one sonnet, for example, Sir Thomas Wyatt circumstantially compares the lover's state to a ship laboring in a storm, and in another he parallels it in detail to the landscape of the Alps. A third sonnet begins with one of the most familiar of Petrarchan conceits, describing the fever and chills of the alternately hopeful and despairing lover (see **oxymoron** under **Figurative language**):

> I find no peace; and all my war is done;
> I fear and hope; I burn, and freeze in ice.

Shakespeare smiled at some of the standard objects pressed into service by Petrarchan writers to describe a lady's beauty, in his sonnet beginning:

> My mistress' eyes are nothing like the sun;
> Coral is far more red than her lips' red:
> If snow be white, why then her breasts are dun;
> If hairs be wires, black wires grow on her head.

The **metaphysical conceit** is a characteristic kind of figure in the poems of John Donne and his followers (see **Metaphysical poets**). It was described by Dr. Johnson, in a famous passage, as "a kind of *discordia concors,* a combination of dissimilar images, or discovery of occult resemblances in things apparently unlike." The metaphysical poets exploited all knowledge—commonplace or esoteric, practical or philosophical, true or fabulous—for these figures; and their comparisons were usually novel, witty, and at their best, startlingly successful. In sharp contrast to conventional Petrarchism, for example, is Donne's "The Canonization," with its extraordinarily inventive sequence of comparisons for the situation of two lovers, moving, as the poetic argument develops, from the area of commerce and business, through various real and mythical birds and diverse forms of historical memorials, to a climax which triumphantly equates the acts and status of physical lovers with the ascetic life and heavenly destination of unworldly saints. The most famous sustained conceit is Donne's comparison of the continuing unity of his soul with his lady's, in spite of their physical parting, to the action of a draughtsman's compass. The passage is in "A Valediction Forbidding Mourning," and begins:

> If they be two, they are two so
>   As stiff twin compasses are two;
> Thy soul, the fixed foot, makes no show
>   To move, but doth if the other do. . . .

Equally well known, but this time as an instance of the grotesque and chilly ingenuity of the unsuccessful metaphysical conceit, is Richard Crashaw's description, in "Saint Mary Magdalene," of the tearful eyes of the repentant Mary Magdalene as

> two faithful fountains
> Two walking baths, two weeping motions,
> Portable and compendious oceans.

Concrete. See **Abstract and Concrete.**

Confidant. See **Chorus.**

Conflict. See **Plot and Character.**

Connotation and Denotation. The denotation of a word, in the usage of critics, is the thing or situation the word specifically refers to; its connotation consists of the associated meanings it implies or suggests. "Home" denotes the place where one lives, but connotes intimacy, privacy, and coziness. "Horse" and "steed" both denote the same quadruped, but "steed" has a different connotation, deriving from the romantic literary contexts in which we commonly find that word used. An expert writer is no less sensitive to the nuances of connotation than to denotative meaning in selecting his words. George Herbert wrote,

> Sweet day, so cool, so calm, so bright,
> The *bridal* of the earth and sky. . . .

The word "marriage," although metrically and denotatively equivalent to "bridal," would have been less apt in this context, because more commonplace in its connotation. Keats, in the passage,

> Charmed magic casements, opening on the foam
> Of perilous seas, in *faery* lands forlorn,

altered his original spelling of "fairy" in order to evoke the connotations of antiquity and of the magic world of Spenser's *Faerie Queene* in the older form, "faery." Compare **Ambiguity.**

A related distinction frequently made since the 1920's is that between **emotive** and **referential** language. Referential language—the language of science and of unemotional exposition—makes neutral assertions about matters of fact. Emotive language—including the language of poetry—may make reference to facts, or represent an object or state of affairs, but it expresses also feelings and attitudes toward the matters referred to. The difference is that between a weather report—"the day is fair and cool, with little wind"—and the passage from Herbert cited above. The distinction was popularized by C. K. Ogden and I. A. Richards in *The Meaning of Meaning* (1923).

Consonance. See **Alliteration.**

Convention and Tradition. In the broadest sense, the word "convention" is applied to any specifically literary device or procedure—that is, any aspect or element in which a work of literature differs from the reality it represents—which is generally accepted by the audience. For example, at a performance of the first part of Shakespeare's *Henry IV* you see a room in a tavern. But on the modern stage the room has only three walls; the fourth has been removed so that you and the other members of the audience may watch what occurs inside. You accept without question this dramatic convention. (In Shakespeare's own theater, the same room was conventionally represented by a platform exposed to the audience on three sides.) Presently Falstaff and Poins depart. Prince Hal, alone, utters his thoughts aloud in blank verse. In real life few men speak their thoughts aloud, and no one puts them in blank verse. In a play, however, it is often convenient to present the condition of mind and to clarify the motives of a character in this way, and the **soliloquy** (see **Dramatic monologue**), as well as the patterning of speech into blank verse, are accepted conventions of the theater. As the play goes on, you find that the action moves almost from one end of England to the other and encompasses nearly a year; yet it is all presented, by convention, on the same stage, and in less than three hours.

The readiness of the audience (often without being aware of the fact) to accept such conventions makes possible **dramatic illusion,** which Coleridge in a famous phrase described as "that willing suspension of disbelief for the moment which constitutes poetic faith," and which permits us to respond to the presented action without raising the question of whether or not it is real. Illusion, of course, is not delusion; this is what Bottom and his friends do not understand when they think that the courtly auditors in *Midsummer Night's Dream* will be frightened by the play they plan to put on:

> Write me a prologue [Bottom says] and let the prologue seem to say, we will do no harm with our swords, and that Pyramus is not kill'd indeed; and for the more better assurance, tell them that I Pyramus am not Pyramus, but Bottom the weaver. This will put them out of fear.

Conventions, in this first sense, are necessary or convenient ways of solving the problems imposed by the physical conditions of a particular medium, such as the stage, in imitating life. The term "convention," however, is frequently used in a more restricted sense to designate an element of a literary work which is taken over from earlier works. Any feature, therefore, which occurs repeatedly in works of literature can be called a convention, whether it is a type of character, a pattern of plot, an idea or theme, a manner of presenting a subject, a stanza form, or a stylistic device. Stock characters, such as the Elizabethan braggart soldier, or all the sad young men of the lost-generation novels of the 1920's, are conventional (see **Stock characters**). It is now just as much a literary convention to be outspoken on sexual matters as it was to be reticent in the Victorian Age. A great many of the items listed in this *Glossary,* since they are recurrent elements or forms, can be called conventions; e.g., the pastoral elegy, the sonnet, the *carpe diem* motif, or the Petrarchan conceit. Even realism and naturalism are as much conventional ways of selecting and rendering subject matter as they are reflections of real life (see **Realism and Naturalism**).

In any literary age we find that a number of writers can be grouped together because they exploit similar conventions in their works. The total set of conventions—of subject matter, forms, techniques, and points of view—characteristic of a group of writers in a period are often called a **tradition.** Accordingly, we speak of the Puritan tradition, the Cavalier tradition, and the metaphysical tradition in the seventeenth century, the neoclassic tradition in the eighteenth century, and the romantic tradition in the nineteenth century. The term "tradition" is also used for a complex set of conventions common to a number of writers in various periods. In this way we speak of the classical tradition, the Neoplatonic tradition, or the pastoral tradition, all of which have appeared in many countries and over a number of centuries. There is nothing either good or bad in conformity to literary conventions or traditions as such; it all depends on how fresh and effective a use the individual writer can make of them. Shakespeare, for example, was in many ways a highly conventional playwright; he was also the greatest. The pastoral elegy (see under **Elegy**), the most convention-bound of literary forms, includes some of the finest lyrics in the language.

As opposed to convention, we use the term **invention** for the inauguration by a writer of new forms or materials or modes of expression, while the resulting work is said to possess **originality.** The history of literature shows a repeated process of innovative writers, such as Donne and Wordsworth, who break away from the reigning conventions to produce original works, only to find that their inventions have been imitated by succeeding writers, and that they have served to establish a new tradition, or set of literary conventions. On this subject see John L. Lowes, *Convention and Revolt in Poetry* (1919), and Robert M. Browne, *Theories of Convention in Contemporary American Criticism* (1956). An essay on the importance of tradition which has greatly influenced contemporary critics and poets is T. S. Eliot's "Tradition and the Individual Talent" (1917).

Couplet. Couplets are lines of poetry rhyming in pairs. Couplets have been composed in all meters, but two are especially common (see **Meter**). One is iambic tetrameter (also called the **octosyllabic couplet**), as employed by Swift in "The Beast's Confession":

> The Ass approaching next, confess'd,
> That in his heart he loved a jest.

But the most widely used couplet form is the iambic pentameter, known as the **heroic couplet.**

The heroic couplet was introduced into English poetry by Geoffrey Chaucer and has been in constant use ever since. It was employed most persistently in the neoclassic period, by some poets almost to the exclusion of other meters. Neoclassic practice imposed various limitations on the form, of which the most important are (1) The inclusion in each line of exactly ten syllables, with limited departure from a strict iambic rhythm. (2) The use of end-stopped lines; a pause often occurs at the end of the first line, and the end of the second line usually marks the end of the sentence, or of an independent unit of syntax. Such a couplet, in which the second line concludes the sense, is called a **closed couplet.** (3) The frequent use of a decided **caesura,** or pause, placed somewhere near the middle of the line, but varied in position to avoid monotony.

The sustained employment of the closed couplet meant that two lines had to serve something of the function of a stanza in neoclassic verse, and one purpose of the caesura was to break the two lines into subunits, in order to maximize the possible interrelations of the parts within a single couplet. Frequently the relationship between the first and second line, or between the two halves of a single line, is one of **antithesis.** That is, there is a balance, or parallelism, of grammatical pattern, but a strong contrast or opposition in the meaning (see also **chiasmus** and **zeugma** under **Rhetorical figures**). The following passage from John Denham's *Cooper's Hill* (1642) is an early example of the artful management of the closed couplet which fascinated neoclassic poets, and served Dryden, Pope, and other writers as a model. A close reading will show the subtle ways in which Denham has achieved diversity and emphasis within the straitness of the closed couplet by the variable positioning of nouns and adjectives, the manipulation of vowel and consonant sounds, the shifts in caesura, and the use of balance and antithesis in the last two lines. The poet is addressing the river Thames:

> O could I flow like thee, and make thy stream
> My great example, as it is my theme!
> Though deep, yet clear; though gentle, yet not dull;
> Strong without rage, without o'erflowing full.

And here is one of the many instances of antithetic structure around a caesura in Pope's *Rape of the Lock:*

> Here Britain's statesmen oft the fall foredoom
> Of foreign tyrants, and of nymphs at home.

Major poets of the Romantic Period (except for Byron) rejected the closure, the balanced syntax, and the antithetic rhetoric of the neoclassic couplet. Compare to the passage from Denham the passage quoted under the entry **Meter** from Keats's *Endymion,* in which the pattern of stresses is variable, the syntax unsymmetrical, and the couplets run on freely, with the rhyme serving to color rather than to stop the verse. See **Neoclassic and Romantic, Stanza,** and (under **Meter**) **caesura, end-stopped line, run-on line.**

Courtesy books. See **Renaissance.**

Criterion. See **Criticism.**

Criticism is concerned with the exposition, analysis, comparison, and evalua tion of works of literature. **Theoretical criticism** undertakes to establish, on the basis of general principles, the distinctions and categories to be applied to literature, and the general **criteria,** or "standards," by which it is to be judged as good or bad. **Practical criticism,** or "applied criticism," brings these elements to bear in the discussion of particular works. Coleridge said:

> I should call that investigation fair and philosophical, in which the critic announces and endeavors to establish the principles, which he holds for the foundation of poetry in general, with the specification of these in their application to the different classes of poetry. Having thus prepared his canons of criticism for praise and condemnation, he would proceed to particularize the most striking passages to which he deems them applicable.

The first sentence describes the theoretical and the second the practical aspect of a total criticism. In his *Biographia Literaria* (1817), Coleridge chose to base his own critical theory on the "faculties of the human mind itself. and their comparative dignity and importance," derived from these principles a number of distinctions, and especially the criteria of "fancy" and "imagination," and then proceeded to apply these distinctions and criteria to the practical task of analyzing and evaluating the poems of Wordsworth.

Practical criticism is sometimes distinguished into **impressionistic** and **judicial criticism.** The impressionistic critic attempts to represent in words the felt qualities of an individual work of art and to express the emotional responses which the work evokes from him as an individual. As Hazlitt put it, "You decide from feeling, and not from reason; that is, from the impression of a number of things on the mind . . . though you may not be able to analyze or account for it in the several particulars"; and Anatole France defined criticism, in the impressionistic mode, as "the adventures of a sensitive soul among masterpieces." (See **Objective and Subjective.**) Judicial criticism, on the other hand, attempts to classify literary works, to analyze a work into its parts and their interrelations, to explain the causes of emotional effects, and to base individual judgments on general criteria. Rarely are the two modes of criticism sharply distinct in practice, but good examples of primarily impressionistic commentary can be found in Longinus (see his characterization of the *Odyssey*), Hazlitt, Pater, and (in our own day) some of the critical essays of E. M. Forster.

Since the appearance of John Crowe Ransom's book, *The New Criticism* (1941), the term **new criticism** has been applied to the critical writings of Cleanth Brooks, Allen Tate, Robert Penn Warren, R. P. Blackmur, and Ransom himself. Often, however, the term has been used more broadly to define a widespread tendency in recent literary criticism, both English and American, which derives in large part from the theory in I. A. Richards' *Principles of Literary Criticism* (1924) and *Science and Poetry* (1926), and from the concepts and evaluations expressed in the earlier critical essays of T. S. Eliot. The new critics differ from one another in many ways, but the following areas of agreement may be listed: (1) A poem, it is held, should be treated qua poem, as an object in itself—in Eliot's words, "primarily as poetry and not another thing"—independently of the biography and intentions of the author, the social conditions at the time of its production, or its psychological or moral effects on the reader. The term **intentional fallacy** is sometimes applied to what is claimed to be the error of using the biographical condition and expressed intention of the author in analyzing or explaining a work, and the term **affective fallacy** to the error of judging the value of a work by its emotional effects on the reader. See W. K. Wimsatt, Jr., and M. C. Beardsley, "The Intentional Fallacy," and "The Affective Fallacy," in Wimsatt's *The Verbal Icon* (1954). (2) The principles of the new criticism are basically semantic. That is, poetry is conceived as a special kind of language which is opposed to the language of science and rational discourse, and the key distinctions employed in the criticism concern the meanings and relations of words, symbols, and images. (3) The distinction between genres (see **Genre**), though casually recognized, is not essential in this criticism. The constitution of any work of literature, whether lyric, dramatic, or narrative, is held to be reducible to words, symbols, "thematic imagery," and "symbolic action" as its primary elements, rather than character, thought, and plot (see **Plot and Character**). These linguistic elements are said to be related as "structure and texture," or in the mode of "tension," "irony," and "paradox," into a "reconciliation of diverse impulses," or an "equilibrium of opposed forces"; and the form of a work, accordingly, whether or not it has characters and plot as well as diction, is said to be primarily a "structure of meanings," and to develop mainly through a play and counterplay of imagery. See **Imagery, Irony, paradox** (under **Figurative language**), **Structure and Texture, Tension.** (4) The practical criticism of the new critics makes large use of **explication,** or the detailed analysis of the meanings, ambiguities (see **Ambiguity**), and interactions of the individual words, images, and passages which are said to combine to make up the "total meaning" of a poem. *Explication de texte* has long been used in the teaching of literature in French schools, but the distinctively modern employment of the method derives from such works as I. A. Richards' *Practical Criticism* (1929) and William Empson's *Seven Types of Ambiguity* (1930). (5) It may be added that a number of new critics are hospitable to the search for "archetypal themes" in literature (see **Archetype**).

A good instance of the theory and practice of the new criticism is Cleanth Brooks's *The Well-Wrought Urn* (1947). Robert W. Stallman's *Critiques and Essays in Criticism, 1920–1948* (1949), is a convenient anthology of modern essays, most of which are in this critical mode.

Dactyl. See **Meter.**

Decadence. Decadence was a European movement, with its chief philosophical headquarters in France; it was represented in England in the 1890's by Oscar Wilde, Arthur Symons, Ernest Dowson, and the artist Aubrey Beardsley. Walter Pater had earlier contributed several basic doctrines to the English Decadents, with his recommendation to crowd one's life with sensations, his concept of "the love of art for art's sake," and his taste for an art possessing "that subtle and delicate sweetness which belongs to a refined and comely decadence." In their search for strange sensations with which to crowd their lives, a number of the Decadents experimented with drugs and various types of illicit or perverse amours; many of them died young, for obvious reasons. For typical products, see the novel, *A Rebours* (1884), by the French writer Huysmans, Oscar Wilde's *The Picture of Dorian Gray* (1891), and the lyrical poems of Ernest Dowson. The influence of some decadent tendencies—the theory of art for art's sake, the radical experimentation with style and literary structure, and the use of symbolism (see **Symbol**)—is still felt in the literature of our day.

Décor. See **Setting.**

Decorum. See **Neoclassic and Romantic** and **Style.**

Denotation. See **Connotation and Denotation.**

Denouement. See **Plot and Character.**

Deus ex machina. See **Plot and Character.**

Dialogue. See **Plot and Character.**

Diction refers to the selection of words, the "vocabulary," used in a work of literature. The arrangement of these words into sentences and larger units constitutes a style (see **Style**). The diction of a work, in verse or prose, can be analyzed under such categories as the degree to which the words are abstract or concrete, Latinate or Anglo-Saxon, colloquial or formal, technical or common, literal or figurative, and according to the precision of denotation and the richness of connotation. See **Abstract and Concrete, Connotation and Denotation, Figurative language.**

In almost all ages poets have employed a diction which includes words and phrases not current in the ordinary conversation of their time. A persistent poetic phenomenon, for example, is the use of **archaism,** or words long since vanished from the vocabulary of common speech. Spenser deliberately exploited such obsolete words in the attempt to develop a suitable diction for *The Faerie Queene,* and until recently many poets continued to say "thou dost," and "I ween," and "methought," but only in verse. The term **poetic diction,** however, is usually applied specifically to the practice of neoclassic writers who, like Thomas Gray, believed that "the language of the age is never the language of poetry" because, by the principle of **decorum,** or fittingness, the poet must adapt his diction to the mode and elevation of a particular genre (see **decorum** under **Neoclassic and Romantic** and **Style,** also **Genre**). Formal satire, for example, because it was a direct commentary on everyday affairs, permitted—indeed required—the use of the language really spoken by an urbane and cultivated gentleman (see **Satire**). But other forms, such as epic, ode, and pastoral, required a special diction to raise the matter to the height of the form. Some characteristics of eighteenth-century poetic diction, in addition to archaism, were its Latinity ("refulgent," "irriguous," "umbrageous"); the frequent personification of abstractions and of inanimate objects (see under **Figurative language**); and the use of circumlocution, or **periphrasis,** to avoid low, technical, or commonplace terms through a roundabout, but more elegant substitute. Examples of periphrasis are James Thomson's "finny tribe" for "fish," and his "from the snowy leg . . . the inverted silk she drew" for "she took off her stocking."

The following stanza from Gray's excellent period piece, "Ode on a Distant Prospect of Eton College" (1747), demonstrates all these devices. Note especially the periphrases by which he has evaded, in the elevated style appropriate to an ode, the use of commonplace words like "swim," or "hoop," or "bat":

> Say, Father Thames, for thou hast seen
> Full many a sprightly race
> Disporting on thy margent green
> The paths of pleasure trace;
> Who foremost now delight to cleave
> With pliant arm thy glassy wave?
> The captive linnet which enthrall?
> What idle progeny succeed
> To chase the rolling circle's speed,
> Or urge the flying ball?

Wordsworth, in his 1800 Preface to the *Lyrical Ballads* and in later writings, attacked this poetic diction as "artificial," "vicious," and "unnatural," and claimed that there is no "essential difference between the language of prose and metrical composition"; but by then the strict theory of decorum had gone by the board. See Thomas Quayle, *Poetic Diction* (1924), and M. H. Abrams, "Wordsworth and Coleridge on Diction and Figures," in *English Institute Essays, 1952.*

Didactic. A didactic work is one designed to demonstrate, or to present in an impressive and persuasive form, a moral, religious, or other thesis or doctrine (see **theme** under **Motif**). Didactic works are to be distinguished from purely imaginative works, which are written, not to propose or enforce a doctrine, but as ends in themselves, for their inherent interest and appeal. A didactic work may present direct statements of doctrine, with proofs and examples (Pope's *Essay on Criticism* and *Essay on Man*). It may also, however, take on the aspect and qualities of an imaginative work by utilizing various devices to translate the doctrine into narrative or dramatic terms (see **Allegory,** and under this general heading, **fable, parable,** and **exemplum**), or by employing a central thesis as the principle which primarily determines the choice of characters and development of the plot (see **Plot and Character**). Spenser's *Faerie Queene* is a didactic allegory; Dante's *Divine Comedy* was designed to present, in a narrative sequence, the major truths about man's moral and theological relations to God; and Milton's *Paradise Lost* can also be called didactic, to the extent that the narrative is organized, as Milton himself said, around the "great argument" to "assert Eternal Providence, And justify the ways of God to men." It will be seen from these examples that "didactic" is a technical distinction, and in no way a derogatory term. Some of our greatest literary masterpieces are didactic, and some purely poetic. The term **propaganda** is sometimes used as the equivalent of "didactic," but it is more useful to reserve "propaganda" for that species of didactic work which undertakes to move the reader to take a position, or to take action, on a particular moral, theological, or political issue of the moment. Harriet Beecher Stowe's *Uncle Tom's Cabin,* Upton Sinclair's *The Jungle,* and George Orwell's *1984* differ from *Paradise Lost* in being propagandistic as well as didactic.

Dirge. See **Elegy.**

Discovery. See **Plot and Character.**

Drama. Drama is the literary form designed for the theater, in which the representation is by actors who impersonate the characters and perform the action and dialogue. In **poetic drama** the dialogue is written in verse instead of prose. For dramatic species, see **Comedy, Tragedy, Chronicle plays, Masque, Miracle and Morality plays;** for dramatic components, **Act, Atmosphere, Chorus, Plot and Character, Setting, soliloquy** and **dramatic illusion** (under **Convention and Tradition**), **Stock Characters;** for dramatic styles and devices, **dramatic irony** (under **Irony**), **Expressionism, Realism and Naturalism, Symbol.**

Dramatic monologue. The dramatic monologue was a poetic form perfected and exploited by Robert Browning, although poems as early as Donne's "Canonization" and "The Flea" exhibit many of its characteristics. Insofar as a dramatic monologue presents a single character speaking, it resembles the **soliloquy,** in which a character in a play utters his thoughts aloud. But in a stage soliloquy, unlike a dramatic monologue, the speaker does not address other characters, or even the audience; the convention is that the audience overhears him talking to himself (see **Convention and Tradition**). In its most complete form as employed by Robert Browning (although even some of Browning's monologues lack one or another of these attributes), the dramatic monologue has the following characteristics: (1) A single person, not the poet himself, is presented speaking at a critical moment: the Bishop is dying, Andrea del Sarto once more attempts wistfully to believe his wife's lies, Fra Lippo Lippi has been caught by the watchmen and must explain that to paint angels is not to be one. (2) This person is addressing one or more other people; but, it has been said, a dramatic monologue is like overhearing one end of a telephone conversation—we know of the auditors' presence, who they are, and what they say or do only by the clues in the discourse of the single speaker. (3) The monologue is contrived so that the main focus is on the interesting temperament or character revealed by the dramatic speaker. For example, although Wordsworth's *Tintern Abbey* is spoken by one person to a silent auditor at a significant moment in his life, it is not, like Browning's "My Last Duchess," a dramatic monologue, both because the speaker seems to be the poet himself, and because what he says is presented for the inherent interest of the evolving thought and feeling, instead of being subordinated to the revelation of the speaker's distinctive character (see **Lyric**).

Tennyson wrote "Ulysses" and other dramatic monologues; the form has also been used by Robert Frost and E. A. Robinson, as well as by T. S. Eliot in "The Love Song of J. Alfred Prufrock." Refer to Robert Langbaum, *The Poetry of Experience: The Dramatic Monologue in the Modern Literary Tradition* (1957).

Dream vision was a conventional narrative frame widely employed by medieval poets. The narrator falls asleep and dreams the events described in the poem; usually he is led by a guide, human or animal, and his experiences are at least in part allegorical (see **Allegory**). One of the greatest of poetic achievements, Dante's *Divine Comedy,* is in the mode of a dream vision, and Chaucer used the form in *The Book of the Duchess, The House of Fame,* and other earlier poems. After the Middle Ages the vogue diminished, but it never died out, as Bunyan's *The Pilgrim's Progress* and Tennyson's "A Dream of Fair Women" bear witness. Writers fall asleep and dream for publication even today.

Duodecimo. See **Folio.**

Eclogue. See **Pastoral.**

Elegy. In Greek and Roman poetry, the elegy was any poem composed in a special elegiac meter; and in English poetry, through the sixteenth century and even later, the term was often applied to any serious meditative poem. In modern critical usage, however, an elegy is a formal and sustained poem lamenting the death of a particular person; examples are Tennyson's *In Memoriam* and W. H. Auden's "At the Grave of Henry James." Sometimes the term is more broadly used, as in Gray's "Elegy Written in a Country Churchyard," for a poem mourning the passing of all men and of the things they love.

The **dirge** is also a poem expressing grief on the occasion of a death, but differs from the elegy in that it is short, less formal, and intended to be sung; examples of the dirge are Shakespeare's "Fear No More the Heat o' the Sun," John Webster's "Call for the Robin Redbreast and the Wren," and William Collins' "A Song from Shakespeare's Cymbeline." Two other terms sometimes employed are **threnody,** the equivalent of a dirge, and **monody,** for a dirge or elegy uttered by a single person: Matthew Arnold called his elegy on A. H. Clough "Thyrsis, A Monody."

An important species of this form is the **pastoral elegy,** which was originated by the Sicilian Greek poets, Theocritus, Bion, and Moschus, and continued by Virgil; it remained current in European poetry through the nineteenth century. The most notable English pastoral elegies are Milton's "Lycidas," Shelley's "Adonais," and Arnold's "Thyrsis." The major conventions established for the type by the early pastoral elegists are illustrated here by references to "Lycidas":

1. The setting is pastoral (see **Pastoral**); that is, the poet and the one he mourns are represented as shepherds in the fields (lines 23–36 and elsewhere).

2. The poet begins by invoking the muses, and in the course of the poem makes reference to other figures from classical mythology (lines 15–22, etc.).

3. All nature joins in mourning the shepherd's death (lines 37–49). This feature is sometimes held to be a survival from the primitive antecedents of the pastoral elegy, the laments for the death of Thammuz, Adonis, or other vegetation deities who died in the autumn to be reborn in the spring.

4. The mourner asks the nymphs or other guardians of the dead poet: "Where were you when death took your beloved?" (lines 50–63).

5. There is a procession of appropriate mourners (lines 88–111).

6. The poet raises questions about the justice of divine dispensation and adverts to the corrupt conditions of his own times (lines 64–84,

113–131). Such passages are sometimes called "digressions," but they are entirely integral to the development of "Lycidas."

7. Post-Renaissance elegies often include an elaborate passage in which appropriate flowers are brought to deck the hearse (lines 133–151).

8. In the closing consolation, the tone changes from grief and despair to joy and assurance, as the elegist realizes that death is the gate to a new and better life (lines 165–185).

Samuel Johnson, who detested both pastoralism and mythology in modern poetry, decried "Lycidas" for "its inherent improbability." But Milton, like the other great writers in this mode, uses the ancient conventions with freshness and power. They give him the ritual he wants for absorbing the individual death into the experience of the race, enable him to maintain a degree of distance and impersonality in facing up to death as the basic condition of life, and add to his single voice the resonance of poets singing other poets dead, through the ages. See **Convention and Tradition,** and refer to Thomas P. Harrison, Jr., *The Pastoral Elegy* (1939).

Elizabethan Age denotes the period of Queen Elizabeth's reign, 1558–1603. This was a great—in drama, the greatest—age of English literature; the age of Marlowe, Sidney, Spenser, Shakespeare, Raleigh, Ben Jonson, and many other extraordinary writers, both of prose and of dramatic, lyric, and narrative poetry. See **Renaissance,** and for some literary developments in this period, see **Chronicle plays, Comedy, Euphuism, Lyric, Sonnet, Tragedy.**

Emotive and Referential language. See **Connotation and Denotation.**

Empathy and Sympathy. Empathy signifies an experience in which we identify ourselves with an object of perception and seem to participate in its physical sensations, especially of posture and motion. The experience is sometimes described metaphorically as "an involuntary projection of ourselves into an object," animate or inanimate. In absorbed contemplation we seem to soar with a hawk or to expand into the graceful proportions of a tree whose branches move with the wind. When Keats said that he habitually becomes "a part of all he sees," and that "if a sparrow comes before my window I take part in its existence and pick about the gravel," he was describing the experience of his intensely empathic nature, although long before the word itself was coined. **Sympathy,** on the other hand, denotes fellow feeling, or emotional identification, with a person when we seem to share his experiences and feelings, whether of grief or joy. Thus we sympathize with Othello, or with the emotional experience, in his first attempt to recite a piece in public, of a beloved child.

In criticism the term "empathic" is applied to a passage in which the reader feels empathy with an object described, and infers that the author felt the same way when he wrote the passage. An example of empathy is Shakespeare's description, in *Venus and Adonis,* of

> the snail, whose tender horns being hit,
> Shrinks backward in his shelly cave with pain,
> And there, all smooth'red up, in shade doth sit,
> Long after fearing to creep forth again.

Another is the description of a wave in Keats's *Endymion,*

> when heav'd anew
> Old ocean rolls a lengthen'd wave to the shore,
> Down whose green back the short-liv'd foam, all hoar,
> Bursts gradual, with a wayward indolence.

On this subject refer to Richard H. Fogle, *The Imagery of Keats and Shelley* (1949), Chap. 4.

Encomiastic poems. See Ode.

End-stopped line. See Meter.

Enjambement. See Meter.

Enlightenment. See Renaissance.

Epic. The epic, or **heroic poem,** is a long narrative poem on a serious subject, related in an elevated style, and centered about an heroic figure on whose actions depends to some degree the fate of a nation or a race. The "traditional," or "primary" epics were shaped from the legends that developed in an heroic age, when a nation was on the move and engaged in military conquest and expansion. In this group belong the *Iliad* and *Odyssey* of the Greek Homer, and the Anglo-Saxon *Beowulf.* The "literary" or "secondary" epics were written by sophisticated craftsmen in deliberate imitation of the earlier form. Of this kind is Virgil's Roman poem, the *Aeneid,* which in turn served as the chief model for Milton's literary epic, *Paradise Lost.* Other poems influenced by the *Aeneid* are sometimes loosely called epic, although they depart radically from the formal qualities of the original; among these are Dante's *Divine Comedy* and Spenser's *Faerie Queene.*

The epic was ranked by Aristotle as second only to tragedy in the hierarchy of genres (see **Genre**) and by Renaissance critics as the highest form of all. It is certainly the most ambitious and most exacting of poetic types, making immense demands on a poet's knowledge, invention, and skill to sustain the scope, grandeur, and variety of a poem that tends to encompass the known world and a large portion of its learning. Despite numerous attempts over three thousand years, we possess only a half dozen or so epics of indubitable greatness. Literary epics commonly have the following features, derived from the traditional epics of Homer (see **Convention and Tradition**):

1. The hero is a figure of great national or international importance. In the *Iliad* he is the great Greek warrior Achilles; in *Paradise Lost* he is Adam, who incorporates in himself the entire race of man.

2. The setting is ample in scale, sometimes world-wide, or even larger. Odysseus wanders over the Mediterranean basin (the whole of the world known to the author), and in Book XI he descends into the underworld. The scope of *Paradise Lost* is cosmic, for it includes heaven, earth, and hell.

3. The action involves heroic deeds in battle, such as the Trojan War, or a long and arduous journey intrepidly accomplished, such as the wanderings of Odysseus on the way to his homeland. *Paradise Lost* includes the war in Heaven, the journey of Satan to discover the newly created world, and his audacious attempt to outwit God by corrupting mankind.

4. In these great actions the gods and other supernatural beings themselves take an interest and an active part—the gods of Olympus in Homer, and Jehovah, Christ, and the angels in *Paradise Lost*. These supernatural agents in an epic used to be—sometimes still are—called the **machinery.**

5. An epic poem is a ceremonial performance and is deliberately given a ceremonial style proportionate to its great subject and architecture. Hence Milton's Latinate diction and stylized syntax, his resounding lists of strange and sonorous names, and his **epic similes,** that is, sustained similes in which the comparison is developed far beyond the specific points of parallel to the primary subject (see **Figurative language** and **Style**):

> They . . . in narrow room
> Throng numberless, like that Pygmean race
> Beyond the Indian mount; or faery elves,
> Whose midnight revels, by a forest side
> Or fountain, some belated peasant sees,
> Or dreams he sees, while overhead the Moon
> Sits arbitress, and nearer to the Earth
> Wheels her pale course.

There are also numerous minor conventions in the epic, including the following:

1. The poet begins by stating his theme, then invokes a Muse to help him in his great undertaking and addresses to the muse an **epic question,** the answer to which inaugurates the narrative proper (*Paradise Lost*, lines 1–49).

2. This narration starts **in medias res,** or in the middle of the action, and at a critical point; the events that happened before the narrative opening are introduced later on. *Paradise Lost* opens with the fallen angels in Hell, gathering their forces and determining on revenge. Not until Books V–VII does the angel Raphael relate to Adam the events in Heaven leading to this situation; and in Books XI–XII, after the Fall, Michael foretells to Adam the future of the world up to Christ's Second Coming. Thus *Paradise Lost,* although focused on the fall of man, encompasses all time, from the creation to the end of the world.

3. There are catalogues of some of the main characters, introduced to the listener in formal detail, such as the procession of fallen angels in Book I of *Paradise Lost.* These characters are later given set speeches, ceremoniously delivered, and revelatory of their diverse temperaments; an example is the great consult of the fallen angels in *Paradise Lost,* Book II.

See **Objective and Subjective,** and consult W. P. Ker, *Epic and Romance* (1897), and E. M. W. Tillyard, *The English Epic and Its Background* (1954).

The **mock epic,** or **mock heroic** poem, is a form of satire in which petty characters and trivial events are made ridiculous by being incongruously presented in all the pomp and ceremony of epic characterization, narration, and style. Dryden's *MacFlecknoe* treats of the elevation of a poetaster to be Crown Prince of Dulness as though it were an episode in an epic poem. In the masterpiece of this form, *The Rape of the Lock,* Pope views through the immense proscenium of the epic a quarrel between the belles and elegants of his day over the theft of a lady's curl. The story is solemnly conducted with all the protocol of the epic, including the ceremonious opening and procedure, a grand style, supernatural "machinery," a voyage at sea, a visit to the underworld, and a heroically scaled battle between the sexes, although with metaphors, hatpins, and snuff for weapons. See **Burlesque and Parody** and **Satire.**

Epigram originally meant an inscription, and was later extended to encompass any very short poem—amorous, elegiac, meditative, complimentary, anecdotal, or satiric—which is polished, terse, and pointed; usually an epigram ends with a surprising or witty turn of thought. Sir John Harington wrote a well-known example:

> Treason doth never prosper. What's the reason?
> Why, if it prosper, none dare call it treason.

Martial, the famous Roman epigrammatist, established the model for many later writers. The epigram was much cultivated in England in the late sixteenth and seventeenth centuries by such poets as Donne, Jonson, and Herrick. The form, as we might expect, flourished in the next century of wit, of polish, and of Pope; many of Pope's couplets, in fact, are detachable epigrams. John Byrom proposed this toast in the eighteenth century, while the exiled Stuarts were still Pretenders to the English throne:

> God bless the King—I mean the Faith's defender!
> God bless (no harm in blessing) the Pretender!
> But who pretender is or who is king—
> God bless us all! that's quite another thing.

And here is one of Coleridge's epigrams, to show that romanticism did not preclude wit.

ON A VOLUNTEER SINGER

> Swans sing before they die—'twere no bad thing
> Should certain persons die before they sing!

In the last century or so, "epigram" has come to mean any neat and witty statement, whether in prose or verse. For prose examples, see **Wit and Humor.** Compare **Lyric** and **Vers de société,** and refer to T. K. Whipple, *Martial and the English Epigram* (1925).

Epithalamion (which is also given the Latin spelling **Epithalamium**) is a poem written to celebrate a marriage. The name in Greek means "at the bridal chamber," for the verses were originally sung at the chamber door of the newly married couple. The first English example was written by Sir Philip Sidney in about 1580. Fifteen years later Edmund Spenser wrote the greatest of English instances of this form, "Epithalamion," as a present to his own bride; the poem combines, with unfailing grace and dignity, classical myth and customs, Christian ritual and allusion, and the local Irish setting. Donne, Jonson, Herrick, and many others composed wedding poems, solemn or ribald, according to the occasion and the poet's temperament. In "A Ballad upon a Wedding" Sir John Suckling wrote an engaging parody of such pieces. The tradition persists. Shelley wrote an "Epithalamium"; Tennyson's *In Memoriam,* although it opens with a funeral, closes with an epithalamion; and more recently A. E. Housman has spoken in the antique idiom of the bridal song in "He is Here, Urania's Son." See Robert H. Case, *English Epithalamies* (1896).

Epode. See **Ode.**

Equivoque. See **Figurative language.**

Essay. The essay is the most flexible and inclusive of literary forms. It can be described as any relatively brief composition in prose which undertakes to discuss a point, or to persuade us to accept a thesis, on any subject whatsoever. (See **Didactic.**) The essay differs from a formal treatise in being addressed to a general audience, instead of to an audience of specialists; as a consequence it discusses its subject in nontechnical fashion, and often with a liberal use of such devices as anecdote, illustration, and humor to augment its appeal. A useful and widely accepted distinction is that between the **formal** and **informal** essay. The formal essay, or **article,** is impersonal; the author writes as an authority on the subject and lays his argument out in orderly and systematic fashion. Examples will be found among the serious articles on current issues in any of the magazines addressed to a thoughtful audience —*The Atlantic Monthly, Harper's,* and so on. The informal essay is personal; the author assumes an intimacy and equality of competence with his audience, and writes in a relaxed, humorous, self-revelatory, and sometimes whimsical fashion. Accessible modern examples are the essays of E. B. White and of other contributors to the *New Yorker.*

Theophrastus, Cicero, Seneca, and Plutarch wrote essays long before the genre was given its name by Montaigne's French *Essais* in 1580. The title meant "attempts," and indicated the tentative and unsystematic nature of his discussions, in contrast to formal philosophical and ethical treatises on the same subjects. Francis Bacon, late in the sixteenth century, inaugurated the English use of the term in his own series of *Essays.* In the eighteenth century Addison and Steele's *Tatler* and *Spectator,* with their many successors, gave to the essay its standard modern vehicle, the literary periodical—earlier essays had been published in books—and so established the form as a major department of literature. In the early nineteenth century the founding of new types of magazines, and their steady proliferation, gave great impetus to the writing of essays; from that time to the present almost every man of letters has been an essayist on at least one occasion. Charles Lamb at that time brought the informal, personal essay to a level that has remained unsurpassed; his was also the age of Hazlitt, Hunt, and De Quincey. In our own time the many periodicals pour out scores of essays each week, but they are largely either of the formal expository type or trivial; the distinguished personal essay has languished.

Among the notable essayists in English, in addition to those already mentioned, are Dryden, Johnson, Fielding, Goldsmith, Macaulay, R. L. Stevenson, Washington Irving, Emerson, Matthew Arnold, and (to mention only one modern) T. S. Eliot. See Hugh Walker, *The English Essay and Essayists* (1915), and W. F. Bryan and R. S. Crane, editors, *The English Familiar Essay* (1916).

Euphony and Cacophony. Euphony is attributed to a passage in which the speech sounds seem pleasant and musical to the ear, as in Keats's

And lucent syrops, tinct with cinnamon;
Manna and dates, in argosy transferred
From Fez; and spiced dainties, everyone,
From silken Samarcand to cedared Lebanon.

Analysis of the passage will show that what strikes us as a purely auditory agreeableness is due as much to the meaning, and to the physical ease of articulating the sound combinations, as to the inherent sweetness of the speech sounds themselves. Similarly, in **cacophony**—the use of seemingly harsh and unmusical sounds—the discordancy is the aggregate effect of the sense, sound, and difficulty of articulation. Cacophony may be an unwanted intrusion in verse, because of a momentary lapse in the poet's attention or skill, as in the unfortunate line of Arnold's "Dover Beach": "Lay like the folds of a bright girdle furled." But cacophony may also be functionally manipulated; for humor, as in Browning's

Rats!
They fought the dogs and killed the cats . . .
Split open the kegs of salted sprats,
Made nests inside men's Sunday hats . . .

or for other effects, as in Hardy's deliberate attempt to express dogged endurance in his *In Tenebris, I:*

I shall not lose old strength
In the lone frost's black length:
Strength long since fled!

See **Alliteration** and **Onomatopeia** for other sound effects in verse.

Euphuism is the name for an elaborate and mannered prose style which had a great vogue in the 1580's, after it was introduced by John Lyly in his didactic prose romance, *Euphues* (1579). The style is sententious (that is, full of moral maxims), persistently uses balanced or antithetical constructions, is heavily alliterative, often in a complex fashion, and is addicted to elaborate similes and parallels, many of which are drawn from mythology and the habits of legendary animals. An example from *Euphues:*

Besides this, a fine wit, a sharp sense, a quick understanding, is able to attain to more in a moment or a very little space than a dull and blockish head in a month, the scythe cutteth far better and smoother than the saw, the wax yieldeth better and sooner to the seal than the steel to the stamp or hammer, the smooth and plain beech is easier to be carved and occupied than the knotty box. . . . I go not about, gentlemen, to inveigh against wit, for then I were witless, but frankly to confess mine own little wit, I have ever thought so superstitiously of wit that I fear I have committed idolatry against wisdom.

This self-conscious style deserved the ridicule Shakespeare gave it in *Love's Labour's Lost* and elsewhere, but it helped, at an important time, to regularize and clarify the grammar of English prose, and to exhibit its rhetorical possibilities. See **Alliteration, antithesis** (under **Couplet**), and **Style.**

Exemplum. See **Allegory.**

Explication of text. See **Criticism.**

Exposition. See **Plot and Character.**

Expressionism is a literary movement which began in Germany before the first World War, reached its height in 1919–1925, and affected especially the American theater. It was a successor to **impressionism,** a movement deriving from the theory and practice of Manet, Degas, Monet, Renoir, and other French painters in the later nineteenth century. Impressionists undertook to represent objects as they appear to the artist in a particular moment and mood, and from a particular vantage point, instead of duplicating exactly their physical properties; in English poetry, impressionism influenced the Imagist poets (see **Imagism**). **Expressionism** takes a farther step in the revolt against realism by exaggerating, dislocating, and breaking the normal time sequence, and otherwise distorting the objects and events of the outer world. Its aim is to represent how the world appears to the troubled, and often abnormal, mind of a character in the work, or else to project into the construction of the work the concepts and attitudes of the artist himself. The departures from standard principles of sequence and construction in T. S. Eliot's poem *The Waste Land,* and in James Joyce's *Ulysses* and *Finnegans Wake* can be regarded as examples of expressionistic techniques (see **Novel**). In drama expressionism objectifies a state of mind by exploiting the resources of modern stage design and lighting, and by stylized acting, as well as by means of the nonrealistic structure, symbolic characters, and specially patterned style of the play itself. Eugene O'Neill's *The Emperor Jones* (1920) projects, in a sequence of symbolic scenes, the individual and racial memories of a terrified modern negro; and Elmer Rice's *The Adding Machine* (1923) expresses the mechanical and sterile world of Mr. Zero, a small cog in the impersonal system of big business.

Though expressionism as a concerted dramatic movement proved too tricky and sensational to endure, it has had a lasting effect on the flexible writing and staging of recent plays such as Thornton Wilder's *Skin of Our Teeth* and Arthur Miller's *Death of a Salesman.* Its influence is also apparent in such familiar motion-picture techniques as memory and dream sequences, special lighting effects, and trick photography. Compare

Realism and Naturalism, and symbolism (under Symbol), and see John Gassner, *The Theatre in Our Times* (1954).

Fable. See Allegory.

Fabliau. See Short story.

Falling action. See Plot and Character.

Farce. See Comedy.

Feminine ending. See Meter; for feminine rhyme, see Rhyme.

Fiction. See Novel.

Figurative language is language which departs from what is taken to be the standard construction, order, and significance of words in order to achieve special meaning or effect. Language which accords with the standard form is called literal, and the various kinds of departures from this standard are called figures of speech. These figures have sometimes been divided into two classes: tropes, meaning "turns," in which words are used with a decided change or extension in their literal meaning, and "figures of thought," in which the departure from the standard is primarily in the arrangement or the rhetorical function of the words, without radical change in their literal meaning. The distinction is not at all a sharp one, but, for convenience, the most commonly identified "tropes" are listed here; other figures will be found under the heading Rhetorical figures.

In a simile a comparison between two essentially different items is expressly indicated by a term such as "like" or "as." A simple example is Burns's "O my love's *like* a red, red rose." (See also Conceit, and epic simile under Epic.) In a metaphor a word which in ordinary usage signifies one kind of thing, quality, or action is applied to another, without express indication of a relation between them. For example, if Burns had chosen to say "O my love *is* a red, red rose" he would have used, technically, a metaphor instead of a simile. Here is a more complex metaphor, from Stephen Spender:

> Eye, gazelle, delicate wanderer,
> Drinker of horizon's fluid line.[1]

It should be noted that a metaphor, like a simile, has two items or subjects: the "principal subject," to which the metaphoric word is applied ("my love" and "eye" in the examples cited), and the "secondary subject,"

[1] From *Collected Poems 1928–1953* by Stephen Spender (New York: Random House, 1955).

or the standard, literal meaning of the metaphoric word itself ("rose" in the first example, and "gazelle," "wanderer," and "drinker" in the second). In a usage now widely adopted, I. A. Richards introduced the term **tenor** for the principal subject and **vehicle** for the secondary subject of a metaphor (*Philosophy of Rhetoric*, 1936, Chaps. 5 and 6). Sometimes the tenor of a metaphor is implied rather than expressed; thus, if one says "That cur is a disgrace to his political party," the verbal context indicates that "cur" is the vehicle for an implied tenor, a man. A **dead metaphor** is one that, like "the leg of a table," is so commonly used that we are no longer aware of a distinction between the two subjects, "leg" as the limb of an animate creature (the vehicle), and one of the supports for a table (the tenor). A dead metaphor, however, is only moribund, and can readily be brought back to life. "Are you a man or a mouse?" someone asked Groucho Marx. He answered, "Throw me a piece of cheese and you'll find out."

Some species of metaphor are frequently given names of their own. In **synecdoche,** a part of something is used to signify the whole; thus we use the term "ten *hands*" for ten workmen, and Milton refers to the corrupt clergy in "Lycidas" as "blind *mouths.*" In **metonymy,** the name of one thing is applied to another thing with which it is closely associated; so "the crown" stands for a king, and the term "Shakespeare" stands for the works that Shakespeare wrote, in the sentence, "I have read all of Shakespeare." A figure related to metaphor is **personification** (or in the Greek term, **prosopopoeia**), in which either an inanimate object or an abstract concept is described as being endowed with human attributes, powers, or feelings (compare **Pathetic fallacy**). Milton wrote:

> Sky loured, and muttering sad thunder, some sad drops
> Wept at completing of the mortal sin.

The personification of abstractions is an excellent poetic device (see, e.g., its use in Keats's ode *To Autumn*) which, however, often became stereotyped in eighteenth-century poetic diction (see **Diction**). Coleridge remembered reading an eighteenth-century ode which began:

> Inoculation! heavenly Maid, descend!

Hyperbole is an extravagant exaggeration of fact, used either for serious or comic effect: "Her eyes opened wide as saucers." For more poetic examples, see Marvell's description of his "vegetable love" in "To His Coy Mistress," or Ben Jonson's compliments to his lady in "Drink to me only with thine eyes." The "tall tale" and "tall talk" of the American Southwest is a form of comic hyperbole. There was the cowboy in an Eastern restaurant who ordered a steak well done. "Do you call this well done?" he roared at the waitress. "I've seen critters hurt worse than that get well!"

A **pun** (in Greek, **paranomasia**) is a play on words that are identical or similar in sound but have sharply diverse meanings; or it is the use of a single word or phrase with two incongruous meanings, both relevant. An example of the latter type, also known as an **equivoque,** is the epitaph on a bank teller:

> He checked his cash, cashed in his checks,
> And left his window. Who is next?

Puns have had serious as well as humorous uses. The Catholic church is founded on the Greek pun in Matthew XVI:18 "Thou art Peter (*Petros*) and upon this rock (*petra*) I will build my church"; and many of Shakespeare's characters pun in serious circumstances. Mercutio, bleeding to death, says, "Ask for me tomorrow and you shall find me a grave man." (Compare **Ambiguity.**) A **paradox** is a statement that seems absurd or self-contradictory, but which turns out to have a tenable and coherent meaning, as in the conclusion to Donne's sonnet on death:

> One short sleep past, we wake eternally,
> And Death shall be no more; *Death, thou shalt die.*

If the paradoxical statement combines two terms that in ordinary usage are contraries, it is sometimes distinguished as an **oxymoron;** for example, Tennyson's

> O *Death* in *Life,* the days that are no more.

Petrarchan sonneteers (see under **Conceit**) were fond of the oxymoron in phrases like "pleasing pains," "I burn and freeze," "loving hate," and so on. Donne exploited the paradox beyond all poets, and some of his poems are paradoxical in the over-all structure as well as in the component statements. "The Canonization," for example, is a long proof, full of local paradoxes, of the paradoxical thesis that profane lovers are saints (see **Metaphysical poets**).

Other figures of speech are treated under **Allegory, antithesis** (under **Couplet**), **Conceit, epic simile** (under **Epic**), **Imagery, Irony, Rhetorical figures.** A convenient treatment of the conventional figures is Sister Miriam Joseph, *Shakespeare's Use of the Arts of Language* (1947). Refer also to S. J. Brown, *The World of Imagery* (1927).

Flashback. See **Plot and Character.**

Folio is a term used to describe the type of leaf used in the **format,** or physical make-up of a book. The printer begins with a large sheet of paper; if the sheet is folded once to form two leaves of four pages, the book is a "folio" (the Latin word for "leaf"). When we talk about "the first Shakespeare folio," for example, we mean a volume published in 1623, containing the first collection of Shakespeare's plays, the leaves of which were made by single folds of the printer's sheet. A sheet folded twice into four leaves makes a **quarto;** a sheet folded three times into eight leaves makes an **octavo.** A **duodecimo** volume is made by dividing a sheet into twelve leaves.

The more leaves into which a single sheet has been divided, the smaller the leaf, so that the type of leaf indicates the size of the book; but only roughly, because the dimensions of the original printer's sheet vary, especially in modern printing. A folio, however, is a very large book; a quarto is the next in size, with a leaf that is nearly square; the third in size, or octavo, is the one most frequently used in modern printing. See Ronald B. McKerrow, *An Introduction to Bibliography* (1928).

Folk tale. See Short story.

Foot. See Meter.

Format. See Folio.

Free verse, or in the French term, **vers libre,** is verse which, although more rhythmic than ordinary prose, is written without a regular metric pattern, and usually without rhyme. Something resembling modern free verse is to be found in the King James translation of the *Psalms* and *Song of Solomon,* Matthew Arnold experimented with free measures, and Walt Whitman startled the literary world by using loosely rhythmic and variable lines in his *Leaves of Grass* (1855). The poets of the 1920's, however, began the modern period of intensive exploitation of this verse. An extreme example, the opening section of a poem by E. E. Cummings, will demonstrate how subtle are the effects possible, especially in the variation of pace, pause, and time, when the verse is released from the necessity of a recurrent foot.

CHANSON INNOCENT[1]

in Just-
spring   when the world is mud-
luscious the little
lame baloonman

whistles   far   and wee

and eddieandbill come
running from marbles and
piracies and it's
spring

See Imagism and Meter.

[1] From *Poems 1923–1954,* published by Harcourt, Brace and Company, Inc. Copyright, 1923, 1951, by E. E. Cummings.

General and Particular. See **Abstract and Concrete.**

Genre is a word imported from France to signify a literary species or, as we now often say, a literary "form." The rubrics under which literary works have been classified are numerous and variable, but the most common names still are such old ones as tragedy, comedy, epic, pastoral, lyric, plus some relative newcomers like novel, essay, and biography. From the Renaissance through most of the eighteenth century the recognized genres, or poetic "kinds" as they were then called, were widely thought to be fixed in the natural order of things, like biological species, and "rules" were promulgated to guide the poet to achieve the proper structure, style, and effect in each kind of poem. At that time the genres were also believed to rank in a hierarchy, ranging from epic and tragedy at the top down to the lyric, epigram, and other trifles at the bottom (see **Neoclassic and Romantic**). The development of new forms such as the novel and the long descriptive poem, the rise in prominence and esteem of lyric poetry, together with important shifts in the bases of critical theory, drastically altered both the conception and ranking of the genres. At present genres are most frequently held to be convenient but rather arbitrary ways to classify literary works, and in much recent criticism the distinction between the genres has ceased to play an essential function (see **Criticism**).

In a totally different sense "genre painting" is sometimes used to describe realistic paintings—or realistic literary descriptions—of commonplace and homely objects or situations; farmyard scenes, for example, or a woman at work in a kitchen.

Gothic novel is a type of fiction which was inaugurated by Horace Walpole's *Castle of Otranto, a Gothic Story* (1764)—written in professed imitation of medieval romances—and which flourished in the latter eighteenth and early nineteenth centuries. The setting of these novels was usually medieval, and often a gloomy castle replete with dungeons and subterranean passages; plentiful use was made of ghosts, mysterious disappearances, and other sensational and supernatural occurrences (which sometimes turned out to have natural explanations); and the principal aim was to evoke chilling terror by exploiting mystery and horror in both atmosphere and events. (See **Atmosphere**, and **melodrama** under **Tragedy**.) Well-known examples are William Beckford's *Vathek* (1786), Ann Radcliffe's *The Mysteries of Udolpho* (1794), Matthew Gregory Lewis' *The Monk* (1797), and Mary Shelley's *Frankenstein* (1817). These novels are now read mainly as period pieces, but they showed the way to the exploitation of terror by greater story-tellers later on, from the Brontë sisters and Edgar Allan Poe through Charles Dickens to William

Faulkner. See **Novel**, and refer to Montague Summers, *The Gothic Quest* (1939), and Eino Railo, *The Haunted Castle* (1927).

Hamartia. See **Tragedy.**

Heroic drama. See **Tragedy.**

Hubris. See **Tragedy.**

Humanism. When a term is employed so loosely and variously as "humanism" is today, it is helpful to refer back to its earlier and more fixed application. The newly-coined Latin word *humanista* (in English, **humanist**) signified in the sixteenth century one who taught or studied or conducted investigations in the *studia humanitatis*, or **humanities**—that is, grammar, rhetoric, history, poetry, and moral philosophy (especially in Greek and Latin authors), as distinguished from other less literary fields such as logic, mathematics, natural philosophy, and theology. Scholarly humanists recovered, edited, and expounded many ancient texts in Greek and Latin unknown to the Middle Ages, and so contributed greatly to the store of materials and ideas characteristic of the Renaissance (see **Renaissance**).

Renaissance humanists also wrote extensive commentaries on Latin and Greek authors, as well as many treatises, dialogues, and narrative works concerned with educational, moral, political, and literary problems. In the nineteenth century a new word, **humanism,** came to be applied to the general view of man and the educational ideas common to the writings of many of these humanists. The humanism of the Renaissance was based largely on such classical writers as Aristotle, Plato, Plutarch, and above all Cicero, and therefore is recognizably a continuation of the ancient educational and cultural tradition which had been called *paideia* by the Greeks and *humanitas* by the Romans. (See H. I. Marrou, *A History of Education in Antiquity.*)

Typically, Renaissance humanism assumed the dignity and privileged position of man in the universe; emphasized the study of classical literature, as against natural philosophy, but for its moral and practical instead of purely aesthetic values; and insisted on the primacy of reason, as opposed to the appetites and passions, in ordering human life. "What is the proper nature of man?" Erasmus wrote. "Surely it is to live the life of reason, for reason is the peculiar prerogative of man." Many humanists also stressed the need for a rounded and harmonious development of man's diverse potentialities, physical and mental, artistic and intellectual, as opposed to a merely technical or specialized training, and they tended to justify the attempt of the individual to realize the full perfection of his own nature by the claim that this made the individual of greater service to the state.

Since with few exceptions Renaissance humanists were professed and pious Christians, they incorporated the ideals inherited from the pagan sages into the frame of Christian beliefs; it has recently become common to refer to this loose structure of assumptions and doctrines as "Christian humanism." The result was to confirm and expand certain elements of traditional Christian doctrine and to minimize the opposing elements. The writings of many Renaissance humanists, for example, ignore or actively oppose the view that man is totally corrupt and crushed by the weight of sin, and is entirely lacking in freedom of the will; the view that there is an absolute conflict between the flesh and the spirit, leading to the concept of extreme asceticism as the only godly way of life; and the monastic ideal of a withdrawal from the affairs of this world for a life of contemplation and of preoccupation with the world hereafter.

The rapid advance in the achievements and prestige of natural science and technology after the sixteenth century sharpened, in many later heirs of the humanistic tradition, the need to defend the traditional role of the humanities in a liberal education against the encroachments of natural philosophy and the practical arts. Milton's little tractate *Of Education* (1644), which is in the direct line of Renaissance theories of pedagogy, allows for the study of the theoretical and applied sciences, as well as for a thorough grounding in classical literature and the traditional *studia humanitatis*. In the following century another schoolmaster and humanist, Dr. Johnson, took exception to the scope Milton had allowed to "physical subjects" in his program:

> But the truth is, that the knowledge of external nature, and the sciences which that knowledge requires or includes, are not the great or the frequent business of the human mind. . . . We are perpetually moralists, but we are geometricians only by chance. . . . The innovators whom I oppose are turning off attention from life to nature. . . . Socrates was rather of opinion, that what we had to learn was, how to do good, and avoid evil.

Matthew Arnold, the great representative of the humanistic viewpoint in the Victorian period, opposed the proposal of Thomas Henry Huxley to surrender to science the predominant role in general education that had hitherto been the prerogative of the humane studies. Many of Arnold's leading ideas are adaptations and restatements of the tenets of the older humanism—his view, for example, that culture is a perfection "of our humanity proper, as distinguished from our animality," and consists of "a harmonious expansion of *all* the powers which make the beauty and worth of human nature"; his emphasis on knowing "the best that is known and thought in the world" and his assumption that much of what is best is in the classical writers; and his conception of poetry and eloquence as "a criticism of life." In our own century the movement of 1910–1930 known as **the New Humanism,** under the leadership of Irving Babbitt and Paul Elmer More, argued powerfully for a return to the classics, to a primarily humanistic education, and to a classical view of moral and literary values, and once again in terms which in many instances are closely related to the ideas of Renaissance humanists. But in our time of democratized higher education and of immense proliferation in the specialized demands of technology and of the natural and social sciences, proponents of a broad humanistic base for general education have been fighting a losing cause. In recent years Latin language and literature has been dropped as a requirement for the degree of Bachelor of Arts, and even of Doctor of Philosophy; and in most of our colleges only the pale specter of the earlier humanistic theory of education survives in the book-requirement that all liberal arts students must take six hours in the area of "the humanities."

Refer to Douglas Bush, *The Renaissance and English Humanism* (1939); P. O. Kristeller, *The Classics and Renaissance Thought* (1955); H. I. Marrou, *A History of Education in Antiquity* (1956). For "the New Humanism" see Irving Babbitt, *Literature and the American College* (1908), and Norman Foerster, editor, *Humanism and America* (1930).

Humor and the **Four Humors.** See **Wit and Humor.**

Hyperbole. See **Figurative language.**

Iamb. See **Meter.**

Idyll. See **Pastoral.**

Imagery. This term is one of the most common in modern criticism, and one of the most ambiguous. Its applications range all the way from "mental pictures" to the total meaning presented by a poem; C. Day Lewis, for example, has said that a poem is "an image composed from a multiplicity of images." Two particular senses of the word, however, are of frequent occurrence:

1. The word "imagery" (i.e., images taken collectively) is used to signify descriptive passages in poetry, especially if the descriptions are vivid and particularized, as in Coleridge's

> The rock shone bright, the kirk no less,
> That stands above the rock:
> The moonlight steeped in silentness
> The steady weathercock.

The term "image" should not be taken to imply a visual reproduction of the scene described; some readers of the passage have visual images, some do not. Also, the description may be of any sensations, not only visual ones. Tennyson, for example, appeals to the senses of smell and hearing, as well as sight, in the lines:

> And many a rose-carnation feeds
> With summer spice the humming air.

2. Still more commonly, "imagery" is now used to signify figurative language, especially metaphors and similes (see **Figurative language**). Recent criticism has gone far beyond older criticism in the emphasis on imagery, in this sense, as the clue to poetic meaning, structure, and effect (see **new criticism** under **Criticism**). Caroline Spurgeon, in *Shakespeare's Imagery and What It Tells Us* (1935), pointed out the frequent presence in Shakespeare's plays of "image-clusters," or recurrent groups of metaphors, such as the combination of dog-fawning–melting candy; she also presented evidence that a number of the individual plays of Shakespeare have characteristic image motifs—one instance is the frequency of the figures of sickness, disease, and corruption in Hamlet (see **Motif**). Since then many critics have joined the hunt for "image patterns" and "thematic imagery" in literature. Some critical extremists even maintain that the implications of the imagery, rather than the literal speech and actions of the characters, constitute the basic plot, or underlying "theme," of many plays, novels, and narrative poems. See, e.g., the critical writings of G. Wilson Knight, and Philip Wheelwright, *The Burning Fountain* (1955).

Imagism was a poetic movement in England and the United States between the years 1909 and 1917, organized as a revolt against what Ezra Pound called the "rather blurry, messy . . . sentimentalistic mannerish" poetry of the nineteenth century. Ezra Pound, the first leader of the movement, was succeeded by Amy Lowell; other leading Imagists were H[ilda] D[oolittle], John Gould Fletcher, F. S. Flint, and Richard Aldington. The imagist manifesto, as voiced in *Some Imagist Poets* (1915), edited by Amy Lowell, declared for a poetry which is free to choose any subject and to create its own rhythms, is expressed in common speech, and presents an image that is hard, clear, and concentrated. The Imagists usually wrote in free verse (see **Free verse**). It seems safe to say that the following example by Ezra Pound exceeds all other imagist poems in the degree of its concentration:

IN A STATION OF THE METRO[1]

> The apparition of these faces in the crowd;
> Petals on a wet, black bough.

The "image" in this and many other imagist poems presents the im-

[1] Copyright 1926, 1952 by Ezra Pound and reprinted by permission of the publisher, New Directions, New York.

pression made by an object on a particular poet in a particular situation, so that this literary movement is related to literary **impressionism** (see under **Expressionism**). Consult Stanley K. Coffman, *Imagism* (1951).

Impressionism. For impressionistic criticism, see **Criticism;** for literary impressionism, see **Expressionism.**

In medias res. See **Epic.**

Incremental repetition. See **Ballad.**

Intentional fallacy. See **Criticism.**

Intrigue. See **Plot and Character.**

Invective. See **Irony.**

Invention. See **Convention and Tradition.**

Invocation. See **Rhetorical figures.**

Irony. "Rhetorical" or "verbal irony" is a mode of speech in which the implied attitudes or evaluation are opposed to those literally expressed. Ostensible praise or approval that implies dispraise or disapproval is more frequent than the converse form. Thus in Pope's *Rape of the Lock*, after Sir Plume, egged on by the ladies, has stammered out his incoherent request for the return of the stolen lock,

> "It grieves me much," replied the Peer again,
> "Who speaks so well should ever speak in vain."

This is a simple bit of irony, because it is obvious in the circumstances that the Peer is far from grieved, and that poor Sir Plume has not spoken at all well. Sometimes, however, the use of irony by Pope and other practitioners is very complex indeed, and the clues to the ironic reversals (especially since the writer lacks a speaker's resort to such ironic indicators as facial expression and vocal intonation) are subtle and difficult. That is why the use of irony by a writer carries an implicit compliment to the intelligence of the reader, who is associated with the knowing minority not taken in by the literal meaning. That is also why so many ironists are misinterpreted and sometimes (like Defoe and Swift) get into serious trouble with the obtuse authorities. Following the intricate maneuvers of a great ironist like Swift or Henry James is an ultimate test of a student's skill in reading.

To keep up a sustainedly ironic document, the writer is apt to utilize the device of a **naive hero,** or of a naive narrator or expositor, whose invincible obtuseness leads him to persist in putting an interpretation on affairs which the smiling reader just as persistently alters or reverses. Examples are Swift's well-meaning but stupid economist who makes the *Modest Proposal* to convert the children of the poverty-stricken Irish into a financial and gastronomic asset, or Swift's stubbornly credulous Gulliver, or the narrator of Fielding's *Jonathan Wild the Great,* or the chief characters of Aldous Huxley's *Antic Hay.*

Irony is related to other rhetorical modes. **Invective** is direct denunciation by the use of derogatory epithets; so Prince Hal calls the rotund Falstaff "this sanguine coward, this bed-presser, this horseback-breaker, this huge hill of flesh. . . ." (It will be noted that in this instance there is an *ironic* undertone of affection, as often when friends resort to name calling in the exuberance of their esteem.) Dryden has described the difference in efficacy between direct depreciation by invective and the indirectness of irony, in which the ironist is able to maintain the advantage of self-control and detachment by leaving it to circumstance to convert his bland compliments into insults:

> How easy is it to call rogue and villain, and that wittily! But how hard to make a man appear a fool, a blockhead, or a knave, without using any of those opprobrious terms! . . . There is still a vast difference between the slovenly butchering of a man, and the fineness of a stroke that separates the head from the body, and leaves it standing in its place.

Sarcasm is a caustic and heavy use of apparent praise for actual dispraise: "Oh, you're just a great guy, a prince—I don't think"; it is the common man's usual form of irony. **Understatement,** or **meiosis,** is the kind of irony which derives from deliberately representing something as much less than it really is. Swift wrote, "Last week I saw a woman flayed, and you will hardly believe how much it altered her appearance for the worse." The effect of meiosis is often comic: "The reports of my death," Mark Twain commented, "are greatly exaggerated." See **Figurative language** and **Satire;** and J. A. K. Thomson, *Irony: An Historical Introduction* (1926).

The word "irony" is also used in a number of extended and non-rhetorical ways. **Socratic irony** takes its name and meaning from Socrates' characteristic assumption, in his philosophical discussions, of an attitude of modesty, ignorance, and readiness to entertain points of view which differ from his own, but invariably turn out to be absurd. **Dramatic irony,** or **tragic irony,** is applied to the words and actions of characters in a play who confidently expect the opposite of what fate holds in store, or who say something that anticipates the tragic outcome, but in a sense very different from the one they intended. (See **Plot and Character.**) The Greek dramatists, especially Sophocles, who based their plots on legends whose outcome was already known to their audience, made frequent use of this device. A concentrated instance of dramatic irony is to be found in the Oriental story of the frightened servant who obtains permission from his master to flee to Samarrah in order to escape Death, who had looked at him strangely in the market place. The master himself encounters Death in the market place and asks him why he had looked so strangely at his servant. "Because," said Death, "I was surprised to see him here. I have an appointment with him this afternoon, in Samarrah." **Cosmic irony,** or the **irony of fate,** is attributed to literary works in which God or Destiny is represented to be manipulating events as though deliberately to frustrate and mock the protagonist. This is a favorite structural device of Thomas Hardy. In his *Tess of the D'Urbervilles* the heroine, having lost her virtue because of her innocence, then loses her happiness because of her honesty, finds it again only through murder, and having been briefly happy, is hanged. Hardy concludes: "The President of the Immortals, in Aeschylean phrase, had ended his sport with Tess." **Romantic irony** is a term used by German writers of the late eighteenth and early nineteenth century to designate a mode of dramatic or narrative writing in which the author builds up and then deliberately breaks down the illusion, by revealing himself to be the wilful creator and manipulator of his characters and their actions (see **dramatic illusion** under **Convention and Tradition**). Byron's great narrative poem, *Don Juan,* constantly employs this device for comic or satiric effect.

In some recent critics we find "irony" used in a greatly extended sense, as a general criterion of literary value. It is claimed that only in poems of an inferior order does the poet commit himself unreservedly to any one attitude or outlook, such as love or admiration or idealism, and that superior poems always include an "ironic" awareness of the opposite and complementary attitudes as well. See **new criticism** (under **Criticism**); also I. A. Richards, *Principles of Literary Criticism* (1924), Chap. 32, and Cleanth Brooks, *The Well-Wrought Urn* (1947).

Jacobean Age refers to the reign of James (in Latin, "Jacobus") I, 1603–1625, which followed the Age of Elizabeth. This was the period, in prose writings, of Bacon, Donne, and the King James translation of the Bible; the period also of Shakespeare's greatest tragedies and tragicomedies, and of major writings by other notable poets and playwrights, including Donne, Jonson, Drayton, Beaumont and Fletcher, Chapman, and Webster. See **Renaissance**.

Lai. See **Short story.**

Lampoon. See **Burlesque and Parody.**

Light verse. See **Vers de société.**

Local color. See **Novel.**

Lyric. Greek writers identified the lyric as a song rendered to the accompaniment of a lyre. The term is now used for any short poem presenting a single speaker (not necessarily the poet himself) who expresses a state of mind involving thought and feeling. Sometimes the term is narrowly applied only to a brief expression of a state of feeling for its inherent interest, such as Shelley's "To Night," or this fine medieval song:

> Fowles in the frith,
> The fisses in the flod.
> And I mon waxe wod;
> Mulch sorwe I walke with
> For best of bon and blod.

In the most common application, however, the term also includes extended poetic expressions of a complex evolution of mind, such as the elegy and ode. Lyrics are distinguished from the other short poetic forms: the epigram merely presents a witty turn of thought, and the ballad, unlike the lyric, has a narrative plot (see **Epigram** and **Ballad**). The expression of thought and feeling in a lyric may be organized in a great variety of ways. For example, in "love lyrics" the lyric speaker may simply reveal his state of mind in an ordered form, as in Burns's "O my love's like a red, red rose"; or he may gallantly elaborate a compliment to his lady (Jonson's "Drink to me only with thine eyes"); or he may deploy an argument to persuade his mistress to take advantage of fleeting youth and opportunity (Marvell's "To His Coy Mistress"). In other types of lyrics, the speaker may be presented in a sustained process of observation and meditation, in which he tries to analyze and resolve an emotional crisis (Wordsworth's "Intimations Ode" and Coleridge's "Dejection"), or he may exhibit his own complex and interesting character by what he says at a revealing moment (Browning's "My Last Duchess").

For subclasses of the lyric, some distinguished by stanza form and others by subject, rendering, or mode of organization, see **Dramatic monologue, Elegy, Ode, Vers de société, Sonnet.** See also Ernest Rhys, *Lyric Poetry* (1913).

Machinery. See **Epic.**

Märchen. See **Short story.**

Manifesto. See **Neoclassic and Romantic.**

Masculine ending. See **Meter;** for **Masculine rhyme,** see **Rhyme.**

Masque. The masque was an elaborate form of court entertainment, combining poetic drama, music, song, dance, costuming, and spectacle, which flourished in the reigns of Elizabeth, James I, and Charles I. A plot—often slight, and for the most part mythological and allegorical—served to bind together these various elements. The play proper was climaxed by the event that gave the form its name—the dance of masked figures in which the audience often joined. In the early seventeenth century the masque drew upon the finest artistic talents of the day, including Ben Jonson for the poetic script and Inigo Jones, the distinguished architect, for the stage machinery. Each lavish production, a riot of music, color, and movement, cost a fortune; the masque was literally the sport of kings and queens, until all drama was brought to an end by the Puritan triumph of 1642. The examples best known today are the masque-within-a-play in the fourth act of Shakespeare's *The Tempest,* and Milton's sage and serious *Comus,* presented at Ludlow Castle in 1634. See Enid Welsford, *The Court Masque* (1927).

Meiosis. See **Irony.**

Melodrama. See **Tragedy.**

Metaphor. See **Figurative language.**

Metaphysical poets. Dryden said in 1693 that John Donne in his poetry "affects the metaphysics"—i.e., employs the terms and abstruse arguments of the Scholastic philosophers—and in 1779 Dr. Johnson extended the term "metaphysical" from Donne to a school of poets, in the acute and balanced critique he incorporated in his "Life of Cowley." The term is now applied to a group of seventeenth-century poets who show signs of influence by Donne's practice, both in secular poetry (Cleveland, Marvell, Cowley) and in religious poetry (Herbert, Vaughan, Crashaw).

Attempts have been made to demonstrate that the metaphysical poets held a philosophical world-view in common, but the term "metaphysical" fits these very diverse writers only if it is used, as Johnson used it, to indicate merely a common poetic style and manner of thought. Donne set the pattern by writing poems which are expressed in a diction and rhythm modeled on the rough give and take of actual speech, which are often organized in the dramatic form of an argument—with his mistress, or an intruding friend, or God, or internally with himself—and which are persistently "witty" in their use of paradox, pun, and startling parallels and distinctions. (See **metaphysical conceit** under **Conceit,** and **pun** and **paradox** under **Figurative language.**) These poets have had some admirers in every age, but they were generally regarded as interesting eccentrics until an astonishing revaluation after World War I elevated Donne to a position near Shakespeare. The movement began with H. J. C. Grierson's Introduction to *Metaphysical Lyrics and Poems of the Seventeenth Century* (1912), was given strong impetus by T. S. Eliot's essays on "The Metaphysical Poets" and "Andrew Marvell" (1921), and has been continued by a host of scholars and writers, including the New Critics (see under **Criticism**). Refer to George Williamson, *The Donne Tradition* (1930), and R. C. Bald, *Donne's Influence in English Literature* (1932).

Meter signifies the recurrence in a poetic line of a regular rhythmic unit. In English the meter of a line is determined mainly by the relations of stronger and weaker stresses in the component syllables. There are three elements which determine where these **stresses,** or **accents,** will fall in a line of poetry. First, and most important, is the *word accent;* in the word "áccent" itself, for example, the first syllable is stressed, the second unstressed. There are in addition many single-syllabled words in the language, and on which of these the stress will fall depends on the *rhetorical accent,* or the emphasis we give a word because of its function and importance in a particular sentence, and the *metrical accent,* which is determined by the pattern of stresses set up earlier in the metrical line or passage. If the metrical accent enforces an alteration of the normal word accent, we get a **wrenched accent.** Wrenching is not always a sign of lack of skill. It was a convention of the folk ballad (e.g., "fair ladié," "far countreé"), and is sometimes used by poets to imitate the effect of the ballad, as in Byron's

> Beware! beware! of the Black Friar.

It is possible to distinguish many degrees of stress in English speech, but the most common and generally useful fashion of analyzing and classifying English meters is to distinguish only two categories of stress in syllables—"stressed" and "unstressed"—and to group syllables into metric feet according to the patterning of these accents. A **foot** is the combination of stressed and unstressed syllables which constitutes the recurrent rhythmic unit of a line. The feet commonly distinguished in English verse are

Iambic: an unstressed followed by a stressed syllable (recall).

Anapestic: two unstressed syllables followed by a stressed syllable (interrupt).

Trochaic: a stressed followed by an unstressed syllable (older).

Dactylic: a stressed followed by two unstressed syllables (openly).

Spondaic: two successive stressed syllables (heartbreak). This foot occurs only occasionally in English, as a variant rather than a standard metric unit.

A metric line is called a **verse.** It is named according to the number of feet composing it:

Monometer: one foot

Dimeter: two feet

Trimeter: three feet

Tetrameter: four feet

Pentameter: five feet

Hexameter: six feet (an **Alexandrine** is a verse of six iambic feet.)

Heptameter: seven feet

To describe the meter of a verse, we name (a) the kind of foot and (b) the number of feet it contains; a line composed of four anapestic feet, for example, is called "anapestic tetrameter," or "four-stress anapestic." To **scan** a passage of poetry is to go through it, verse by verse, indicating the nature of the component feet. Here are the first five lines from Keats's *Endymion*, with the **scansion** indicated by conventional symbols:

1. A thing of beauty is a joy forever:

2. Its loveliness increases; // it will never

3. Pass into nothingness; // but still will keep

4. A bower quiet for us, // and a sleep

5. Full of sweet dreams, and health, and quiet breathing.

The basic meter is iambic pentameter. As in all freely composed verse, however, there are variations upon the basic foot. Lines 1, 2, and 5 end with an extra unstressed syllable which is called a **feminine ending;** lines 3 and 4, which end with a stressed syllable, have **masculine endings.** In lines 3 and 5, moreover, a trochee has been "substituted" for the initial iamb. It should be added that an expressive reading does not accord mechanically with these markings (the first line, e.g., would probably be read, "A thing of beauty is a joy forever"); nor will any two readers, for that matter, read these lines in precisely the same way. Nevertheless, the *possibility* of scansion into regularly iambic feet is felt as a structural pattern of pulses underlying a more freely expressive rendering of these lines. Also, much English versification that undertakes to render the cadence of the living voice, such as in the later plays of Shakespeare and in many lyrics by Donne and Browning, freely introduces an extra unstressed syllable before the stressed syllables. There is no point in distinguishing such feet as anapestic "substitutions," since the two unstressed syllables are meant to be run over in the reading without breaking the basic iambic movement.

Two other elements which affect the movement of Keats's lines may be mentioned here. In lines 1 and 5, the natural pause in the reading, which comes at the conclusion of a phrase, a clause, or a sentence, coincides with the end of the line, and these lines are called **end-stopped.** Lines 2–4, on the other hand, are called **run-on lines,** because the phrase carries on over the end of the verses. The use of run-on lines is signified by a French term, **enjambement.** When the phrasal pause falls within the line, as in lines 2, 3, and 4, it is called a **caesura,** indicated in the quoted passage by the conventional symbol, //. The management of the caesura, always important for giving variety and rhetorical emphasis in the long pentameter line, is of particular importance in the narrow limits of the closed couplet (see **Couplet**).

Quantitative meters in English are written in imitation of Greek and Latin versification, in which the rhythm depended, not on stress, but on the "quantity," or duration of pronunciation, of a syllable, and the foot consisted of a combination of "long" and "short" syllables. Sidney, Spenser, and other poets in the Elizabethan period experimented with the possibility of substituting quantitative measures for standard English accentual verse; Coleridge, Tennyson, and Longfellow are among the later poets who have written English imitations of classical meters. **Sprung rhythm** was G. M. Hopkins' term for a mixed meter in which the foot consists of a stressed syllable which may stand alone, or may be combined with from one to three or more unstressed syllables (see Hopkins' "The Windhover"). If the rhythm of a poem does not contain any recurrent foot, or unit of stress pattern, it is called **free verse** (see **Free verse**).

R. M. Alden's *English Verse* (1903) is a well-illustrated treatment of conventional English metrics. Later metrical theories are described in T. S. Omond, *English Metrists* (1921) and George R. Stewart, *The Technique of English Verse* (1930). See also **Rhyme** and **Stanza.**

Metonymy. See **Figurative language.**

Miracle and Morality plays were types of medieval verse drama. The **miracle play** took its subject matter from Biblical history or from the legends of the saints. (In the usage of some historians, however, "miracle play" is used only for drama based on the life of a saint, and the term **mystery play** is applied to dramatized episodes from the Old and New Testament.) The Biblical plays were usually performed on religious festivals in great "cycles," covering the history of man from the Creation to the Last Judgment. For examples of the way in which the Biblical material was expanded and comic episodes inserted, see "Noah" and the "Second Shepherd's Play" in the Wakefield cycle. A **morality play** was an allegory on the Christian way of life, in which some of the chief characters were personifications of virtues and vices, engaged in a struggle for the soul of mankind (see **Allegory**). The best-known, and also the best, of these plays is *Everyman* (fifteenth century). See A. W. Pollard, *English Miracle Plays, Moralities, and Interludes* (1923), and Hardin Craig, *English Religious Drama of the Middle Ages* (1955).

Mock epic. See **Epic, Burlesque and Parody,** and **Satire.**

Monody. See **Elegy.**

Morality play. See **Miracle and Morality plays.**

Motif is a term now applied to a frequently recurrent character, incident, or concept in folklore or in literature. The "loathly lady" who turns out to be a beautiful princess is a folklore motif. The man fatally bewitched by a fairy lady is a motif adapted from folklore in Keats's "La Belle Dame sans Merci." Examples of motifs common in lyric poems are the **ubi sunt** motif, or "where-are" formula for lamenting the vanished past ("Where are the snows of yesteryear?"), and the **carpe diem,** or "seize-the-day" motif, whose nature is sufficiently indicated by Herrick's title, "To the Virgins, to Make Much of Time." The term "motif" is also applied to the deliberate repetition of a significant phrase in a single work, as in the operas of Richard Wagner and the novels of Thomas Mann, James Joyce, and Virginia Woolf. See also **Archetype** and **Stock characters.**

A motif is sometimes called a **theme,** but the word "theme" is more usefully employed to denote the thesis or doctrine of a didactic work (see **Didactic**). The broad theme of the *Essay on Man*, for example, as Pope states it, is to

> Laugh where we must, be candid where we can,
> But vindicate the ways of God to man.

In modern criticism, the word "theme" is often used also to signify the abstract concept which is said to be embodied in the structure and imagery of a nondidactic or purely imaginative work. It has been said, for example, that the theme of Keats's "Ode to a Nightingale" is "man's inability to correlate finally the ideal and the actual aspects of existence." This proposition undoubtedly has some relation to the matter of the poem, but it is not very helpful to speak of it as the "theme" of the work, and to do so can easily be misleading, for several reasons. Various other abstract statements would fit Keats's poem just as well as this one; the statement is so general that it could apply equally well to an indefinite number of other poems; and, above all, it certainly does not function, like the theme of a didactic work, as the doctrine which the whole poem is designed to clarify and make persuasive to the reader.

Motivation. See **Plot and Character.**

Mystery play. See **Miracle and Morality plays.**

Myth. In its primary significance a myth is one story in a **mythology,** or system of narratives, which were once widely believed to be true, and which served to explain, in terms of the intentions and actions of supernatural beings, why the world is what it is and why things happen as they do. One way of putting it is to say that a mythology is a religion in which we no longer believe. Poets, however, long after they ceased to believe in the historical truth of these tales, have persisted in using the myths of Jove, Hercules, Prometheus, and Wotan for allusions, episodes, or plots; as Coleridge said, "still doth the old instinct bring back the old names." The term "myth" has also been extended in various ways. Plato used "myth," or accounts of supernatural beings and actions that he invented himself, in order to project philosophical speculation beyond the point at which it is possible to have certain knowledge; see, e.g., the "Myth of Er" in Book X of *The Republic.* Some German romantic critics proposed that to write great poetry, modern poets must deliberately invent for themselves a central and unifying "mythology," analogous to the genuine, or hereditary, mythologies of the past. In the same period in England, William Blake, who felt "I must create a system or be enslaved by another man's," presented in his poems a mythology constructed by fusing his own intuitions and visions with fragments from traditional legends. A number of modern critics, like the Germans earlier, have affirmed that myth, whether inherited or invented, is essential to poetry. Yeats is the chief modern example of a poet who undertook to construct a mythology of his own, which he expounded in *A Vision* (1926) and employed as the basis for a number of great lyric poems.

Myth is a very prominent word in modern criticism where, in addition to the meanings already described, it exhibits a variety of other meanings ranging all the way from a widely held fallacy (we speak, e.g., of "the myth of progress" and "the American success myth") to a solidly imagined, though fictitious, milieu in which the action of a literary work is represented as taking place ("Faulkner's myth of Yoknapatawpha County," "the mythical world of *Moby Dick*"). See also **Allegory** and **Archetype,** and consult H. J. Rose, *A Handbook of Greek Mythology* (1939); and Douglas Bush's two books, *Mythology and the Renaissance Tradition in English Poetry* (1933), and *Mythology and the Romantic Tradition in English Poetry* (1937). For examples of the uses of the term in recent criticism, see

Kimon Friar and J. M. Brinnin, *Modern Poetry* (1951), and Philip Wheelwright, *The Burning Fountain* (1954).

Naturalism. See **Realism and Naturalism.**

Negative capability. See **Objective and Subjective.**

Neoclassic and Romantic. The simplest and safest use of the troublesome terms "neoclassic" and "romantic" is as noncommittal names for literary periods. In this application, neoclassic literature is the literature written in the century or so between Dryden and Dr. Johnson, and romantic literature is the literature written in approximately the first three decades of the nineteenth century. Historians have often, in addition, tried to "define" neoclassicism or romanticism, conceived as essences or pervasive somethings which give their distinctive quality to these literatures. Unfortunately, literary history does not seem to have formed itself around such single concepts, however convenient that might have been for the historian. The numerous and conflicting single "definitions" of neoclassicism and romanticism are either so vague as to be next to meaningless or so specific as not to apply to the range and variety of the literary facts.

A more useful undertaking is to try to specify some attributes of literary theory and practice, common to a number of important writers in a given period, which serve to differentiate these writers from those of other periods. The following list of ideas and characteristics shared by such authors as Dryden, Pope, Addison, Swift, Johnson, and Goldsmith may be useful to the student as an introductory outline of **neoclassicism,** provided that he be alert to qualify these generalizations according to the special concepts and qualities he finds in each individual writer:

1. These authors exhibited a strong traditionalism, often joined with a distrust of radical innovation, and shown above all in a great respect for classical writers (especially Roman writers) as having established the models and precepts for most of the major literary genres (see **Genre**). Hence the term "neoclassic."

2. A reigning concept was that literature is primarily an "art," demanding indeed innate talents, but perfected only by long study and practice, and consisting in the adaptation of known and tested means to the achievement of foreseen ends upon the audience of readers. The neoclassic ideal is the craftsman's ideal, demanding the utmost finish, elimination, correction, and attention to detail. Special allowances were often made for the unerring freedom of "natural geniuses," and for those happy strokes, available even to some less gifted poets, which occur without premeditation and achieve, as Pope said, "a grace beyond the reach of art." But the natural genius like Homer or Shakespeare is a rarity, and

probably a thing of the past, and literary "graces" come only occasionally. The neoclassic writer strove, therefore, for "correctness," and usually he respected the **rules**. The **rules** were properties, abstracted from classic writings whose long survival has proved their excellence; these properties, many critics believed, must be embodied in modern works if they, too, are to be excellent and to survive. (See **decorum** under **Style, Diction,** and the **unities** under **Plot and Character**.)

3. Man, and especially man as an integral part of an organized society, was regarded as the primary, although not the sole, source of poetic subject matter. And poetry, by the human actions it imitates, and the artistic form it gives to the imitation, was designed to yield both instruction and aesthetic pleasure to the men who read it. Not art for art's sake, but art for *man's* sake was the ideal of neoclassic humanism.

4. Both in the subject matter and appeal of art, emphasis was placed on what men possess in common—representative characteristics, and widely shared experiences, thoughts, and tastes. "True wit," Pope said in a much-quoted passage, is "what oft was thought but ne'er so well expressed." That is, a primary aim of poetry is to give new and perfect expression to the great commonplaces of human wisdom, whose prevalence and durability are the best warrant of their importance and truth. There was also insistence, it should be noted, on the need to balance or enhance the typical and the familiar with the opposing qualities of novelty, particularity, and invention. Johnson substituted for Pope's definition of true wit the statement that it "is at once natural and *new*," and praised Shakespeare because, while his characters are all species, they are all "discriminated" and "distinct." But there was wide agreement that the general nature of mankind is the basic source and test of art.

5. Neoclassic writers, like the philosophers of the time, viewed man as a limited being who ought to address himself to accessible goals. Many of the great works of the period, satiric and didactic, attack man's "pride," or presumption beyond the natural limits of his species, and enforce the lesson of the golden mean, the avoidance of extremes, and of man's need to submit to his restricted position in the order of things. In art, as in life, there prevailed the law of measure and the acceptance of strict limits upon one's freedom. The poets admired excessively the great genres of epic and tragedy but wrote their own masterpieces in admittedly lesser forms such as the verse essay, and especially satire, in which they had more chance to equal or surpass their English predecessors (see **Genre** and **Satire**). These poets gladly submitted to various rules and limiting conventions in their subjects, structure, and diction. Typical was their election, in many of their poems, to write within the extremely tight restrictions of the closed couplet (see **Couplet**). But the essence of the urbane and civilized poetry of the neoclassic period

is "the art that hides art"; that is, the seeming freedom and triumphant ease with which it meets the challenge set by traditional and drastically restrictive patterns.

Here are some aspects in which **romantic** ideals and writings in the first three decades of the nineteenth century differ most conspicuously from the neoclassic:

1. The prevailing attitude favored innovation instead of traditionalism in the materials, forms, and style of literature, and without regard to classical precedent. The romantic period began with a kind of **manifesto,** or statement of revolutionary aims, in the Preface to the second edition of Wordsworth's and Coleridge's *Lyrical Ballads* (1800). This Preface, written by Wordsworth, denounced the poetic diction of the preceding century and proposed to deal with materials from "common life" in "a selection of language really used by men." The serious or tragic treatment of lowly subjects in common language violated the basic neoclassic rule of **decorum,** or propriety, which asserted that the serious genres should deal with high subjects in an appropriately elevated style (see **Diction** and **Style**). Other innovations in the period were the exploitation by Coleridge, Keats, and others of the realm of the supernatural and of "the far away and the long ago," and the use of symbolist techniques by Blake and Shelley (see under **Symbol**).

2. In his Preface Wordsworth defined poetry as "the spontaneous overflow of powerful feelings." From this point of view the essential element of poetry is not men in action but the poet's own feelings, while its composition, being "spontaneous," is the opposite of the artful manipulation of means to foreseen ends emphasized by the neoclassic critics. Wordsworth continuously appealed from "artificial" rules and conventions to "nature" as the criterion of poetry (see **Primitivism**), and Coleridge opposed to the neoclassic rules, imposed from without, the concept of organic "laws," by which each poetic work evolves, according to its own inherent principles, into its final form.

3. External nature to an extraordinary degree displaced humanity as a primary element of poetic subject matter. In their major poems, even those that are meditative or narrative rather than descriptive, Wordsworth and Coleridge—and to a lesser extent Keats and Shelley—usually set out from and return to an aspect or change of aspect in the landscape.

4. Neoclassic poetry was about other men, but romantic poetry, when it concerned man rather than nature, was often about the poet himself. (See **Objective and Subjective.**) And whether the romantic subject was the poet or someone else, he was no longer an integral part of an organized society but typically a solitary figure, and often a social nonconformist or outcast. Many major romantic works had as protagonist the rebel, whether for good or ill: Prometheus, Cain, the Satanic hero, or the great outlaw.

5. Many romantic writers viewed man as a being of immense potentialities, in touch with the infinite through an intuitive faculty which they
called either Reason or Imagination. "Our destiny," said Wordsworth,
"our being's heart and home, is with infinitude, and only there." The
neoclassic emphasis on the complete achievement of finite aims was
replaced by a widespread dissatisfaction with imposed limits and restrictions; success was often held to lie in the intrepid attempt beyond bounds;
and the earlier satisfaction in the perfectly accomplished, because limited,
undertaking gave way to a preference for the glory of the imperfect.
Romantic writers once more undertook to compete with their greatest
predecessors in audacious and exacting long poems: Wordsworth's
Prelude, Blake's "prophetic" poems, Shelley's *Prometheus Unbound,*
Keats's *Hyperion,* Byron's *Don Juan.*

Refer to A. O. Lovejoy, *Essays in the History of Ideas* (1948); René
Wellek, "The Concept of 'Romanticism' in Literary History," *Comparative
Literature* (I, 1949); W. J. Bate, *From Classic to Romantic* (1948); M. H.
Abrams, *The Mirror and the Lamp: Romantic Theory and the Critical
Tradition* (1953).

New Criticism. See **Criticism.**

Novel. The term is now applied to a great variety of writings which have
in common only the attribute of being an extended piece of prose fiction.
As fiction the novel is distinguished from history, which undertakes to
be a narrative of facts, and from the essay, which often presents characters and incidents (as Addison does in the *Spectator* papers), but only as
a brief illustration of a concept or point of view. As an extended narrative
covering a wide range of characters and experience, the novel differs
from the short story; and as prose, it differs from the long verse narratives
which, since the end of the seventeenth century, it has gradually sup-
planted. Within these limits the novel nevertheless includes such diverse
works as Richardson's *Pamela* and Hemingway's *The Sun Also Rises,*
Cooper's *The Deerslayer* and Henry James's *The Wings of the Dove,*
Dickens' *Pickwick Papers* and Joyce's *Ulysses.*

The novel is the modern equivalent of various earlier forms of the
extended narrative. The first of these, the epic (see **Epic**), was succeeded
in the Middle Ages by the **romance,** written at first, like the epic, in verse
but later in prose as well. The romance related the adventures of kings
and knights, introduced a heroine and made love a major interest, and
moved the realm of the supernatural from Olympus to fairyland. Supernatural events in the epic had their causes in the will and actions of the
gods; in romances, such events are mysteriously effected by magic, spells,
and enchantments. *Gawain and the Green Knight* is a fourteenth-century
verse romance, and Malory's *Morte d'Arthur* is a fifteenth-century prose

rendering of the many earlier verse romances centering around the legendary King Arthur and the knights of the Round Table. The word "romance" eventually yielded the word *roman,* which is the term for the novel in most European languages. The English name for the form, however, is derived from the Italian **novella** (meaning "a little new thing"), which was a short prose tale. In fourteenth-century Italy there was a great vogue for collections of *novelle,* some serious and some scandalous; the best known of these collections is Boccaccio's *Decameron,* still available in any well-stocked bookstore (see **Short story**).

Another important predecessor of the novel was the **picaresque story,** which developed in sixteenth-century Spain, although the most popular example, *Gil Blas* (1715), was written by the Frenchman Le Sage. *Picaro* is Spanish for "rogue," and the typical story has for its subject the escapades of a merry rascal who lives by his wits; it is realistic in manner, episodic in structure, and often satiric in aim. The development of the novel owes much to works which were written as realistic antitypes, in order to deflate romantic or idealized fictional forms. Many *novelle,* as well as the picaresque stories, were of this sort, and Cervantes' *Don Quixote* (1605), a quasi-picaresque satire on the outmoded ideals of the chivalrous romance, is the greatest single progenitor of the modern novel.

After these precedents and many others, including the pastoral romance (see **Pastoral**) and the seventeenth-century **character** (brief sketches of people representing a type of personality or a way of life), the novel as we now think of it emerged in England in the early eighteenth century. In 1719 Defoe wrote *Robinson Crusoe,* and in 1722 *Moll Flanders.* Both of these are picaresque in type, in the sense that they are a sequence of episodes held together largely because they happened to one person, and Moll is herself a colorful female version of the old *picaro*—"twelve year a Whore, five times a Wife (whereof once to her own Brother), Twelve year a thief, Eight year a Transported Felon in Virginia," as the title page resoundingly informs us. But *Robinson Crusoe* is given an apparent unity of action by the accident of shipwreck, which focuses the plot on the problem of survival on an uninhabited island, while both stories present so convincing a central character, set in so solid and factually realized a world, that Defoe is often credited with writing the first true novels of incident.

The credit for having written the first novel of character is more nearly unanimously given to Samuel Richardson for his *Pamela; or, Virtue Rewarded* (1740). *Pamela* is the story of a sentimental but shrewd young servant girl who, by prudently safeguarding her virtue, becomes the wife instead of the mistress of a wild young gentleman, and therefore a lady instead of a debauched serving maid. This, like its greater and tragic successor, *Clarissa Harlowe* (1747–1748), is an **epistolary novel;** that is, the narrative is conveyed entirely in exchanges of letters. The distinction between the novel of incident and the novel of character cannot be drawn sharply, for as Henry James has said, "What is character but the determination of incident? What is incident but the illustration of character?" But in the novel of incident, the weight of interest is on what the character will do next and on how the plot will come out; in the novel of character, it is on his motives for what he does and on how he as a person will turn out.

Since its flowering time in the Victorian period, the novel has displaced all other literary forms in popularity, and has replaced long verse narratives almost entirely. The art of the novel has received the devoted attention of some of the greatest craftsmen in modern literature—Flaubert, Henry James, Proust, Mann, and Joyce. There has been constant experimentation in techniques, especially in the manipulation of the time sequence, in point of view (see **Point of view**), and in the use of symbolism (see **Expressionism** and **Symbol**). Henry James's Prefaces, republished as *The Art of the Novel* (1934), will exemplify the subtlety and care that has been lavished upon the novelist's craft; while the novels of Proust, Joyce, Mann, and Virginia Woolf will show how radical—and successful—have been modern innovations in form, sequence, and the interrelations of parts. One prominent modern development, characteristic of the attempt to probe ever deeper into the interior life of the characters, is the use of the technique called **stream of consciousness.** Long passages of introspection are found in earlier novelists such as Dostoevski and Henry James, but the technique proper undertakes to reproduce the raw flow of consciousness, with its perceptions, thoughts, judgments, feelings, associations, and memories presented just as they occur, without being tidied into grammatical sentences or given logical and narrative order by the novelist. The method is sometimes described as the exact reproduction of consciousness; but since sense perceptions, feelings, and even aspects of thought are nonverbal, it is clear that the author must convert these elements into words, and much of this conversion is a matter of convention rather than of point-by-point reproduction. James Joyce perfected the technique in *Ulysses* (1922); see, e.g., the 42-page "interior monologue" of Molly Bloom with which the novel ends. Stream of consciousness is used occasionally by Virginia Woolf, William Faulkner, and others, and in the many volumes of her novel, *Pilgrimage*, by Dorothy M. Richardson. Refer to Melvin J. Friedman, *Stream of Consciousness* (1955).

Types of novels are often distinguished on the basis of differences in subject matter, mode of presentation, or purpose. The **sociological novel,** for example, emphasizes the influence of economic and social conditions on characters and events, and often embodies an implicit thesis for social reform (H. B. Stowe's *Uncle Tom's Cabin*, John Steinbeck's *Grapes of Wrath*); see **Didactic.** The **historical novel** takes its setting and a number of its characters and events from history, and utilizes the historical element either for picturesque adventure, or for antiquarian interest, or for both (Scott's *Ivanhoe*, Kenneth Roberts' *Northwest Passage*). The **regional novel** emphasizes the setting and mores of a particular locality, as these affect character and action ("Wessex" in Hardy's novels, or the State of Mississippi in Faulkner's); see **Setting**. If the regional setting, including landscape, dialect, and customs, is exploited particularly for its inherent interest and oddity, it is often referred to as **local color** (India in Kipling's novels and stories, or the South in Erskine Caldwell's).

For additional topics related to the novel, see **Atmosphere, Comedy, Didactic, Gothic novel, Plot and Character, Realism and Naturalism, sentimental novel** (under **Sensibility and Sentimentalism**), **Short story, Stock characters, Tragedy**. See also Percy Lubbock, *The Craft of Fiction* (1921); Edwin Muir, *The Structure of the Novel* (1928); E. A. Baker, *History of the English Novel* (1924 ff.); W. E. Allen, *The English Novel* (1954).

Novelette. See **Short story.**

Novella. See **Novel** and **Short story.**

Objective correlative is a term rather casually introduced by T. S. Eliot in an essay on *Hamlet* (1919), whose subsequent vogue, Eliot has confessed, astonished its inventor. "The only way of expressing emotion in the form of art is by finding an 'objective correlative'; in other words, a set of objects, a situation, a chain of events which shall be the formula of that *particular* emotion; such that when the external facts, which must terminate in sensory experience, are given, the emotion is immediately evoked." In Lady Macbeth's sleepwalking speech, and in Macbeth's speech on hearing of his wife's death, according to Eliot, the words are completely adequate to the state of mind. Hamlet, however, "is dominated by an emotion which is inexpressible, because it is in *excess* of the facts as they appear" ("Hamlet," in *Selected Essays*, 1932.)

Objective and Subjective. John Ruskin complained in 1856 that "German dulness and English affectation have of late much multiplied among us the use of two of the most objectionable words that were ever coined by the troublesomeness of metaphysicians—namely, 'Objective' and 'Subjective.'" Ruskin was at least in part right. The words were imported into England from the post-Kantian German critics of the latter eighteenth century, and they are certainly troublesome. There is one relatively simple usage, in which "subjective" is applied to narratives where the emphasis is on character, motive, and facts of mind, rather than on external action (compare "novels of character" under **Novel**). "Subjective," however, is more frequently used to signify literature into which the writer himself projects his private experiences, disposition, and feelings; "objective," to signify literature in which the poet merely presents his invented characters and their thoughts, feeling, and actions, himself remaining aloof, noncommittal, and uninvolved. On this distinction most critics agree; but there is little agreement as to what writers, periods, and works are properly to be labeled with the one or other of these contrary terms.

At an extreme, some critics maintain that all genuine literature is subjective and that Shakespeare, for example, or Milton, has projected aspects of his own temperament into many, or even all, of his characters. But this application of the term attributes to poets a kind of schizophrenia and, at any rate, by extending its reference to all works of literature, makes the term useless for criticism. Most critics, however, agree in saying that Shakespeare is an objective dramatist, who presents his imagined characters in action without expressing his own personality or obtruding his own inclinations or judgments. This objectivity is what Keats meant by speaking of Shakespeare's **negative capability,** and what more recent critics often mean by **aesthetic distance.** Epic poets traditionally narrate events in the first person. "Arms and the man *I* sing," Virgil began, and Milton prays to the Heavenly Muse for inspiration, that "*I* may assert Eternal Providence." But the epic poet, as Coleridge said, "is a mere voice"—a public voice, assumed for ceremonial purposes, and not the private voice of Virgil or Milton in their everyday persons. We say, therefore, that an epic poet is objective (see **Epic**). On the other hand, Milton, unlike Virgil, introduces some books of his epic by discoursing about his own blindness and other personal circumstances, and these single passages of *Paradise Lost,* although elevated and formal, may properly be called subjective. Wordsworth's *Prelude* is a poem of epic length and seriousness which is thoroughly subjective, because the speaker of it is admittedly Wordsworth himself, telling about his life and feelings and poetic development. The degree to which Wordsworth and his contemporaries, by their own admission, grounded many of their poems on personal experiences lies behind the frequent statement that the romantic period is a subjective age. (See **Neoclassic and Romantic.**) A number of modern quasi-autobiographical novels, such as Joyce's *Portrait of the Artist as a Young Man* and Thomas Wolfe's *Look Homeward Angel,* are also subjective in this sense.

It is often said that all lyric poetry is subjective because it is written in the first person (see **Lyric**). But there is no reason why the "I" of Shakespeare's sonnets need be Shakespeare himself rather than a fictitious lyric speaker; after all, none of us assumes that the speaker who begins a lyric poem, "That's my last Duchess painted on the wall," is Robert Browning masquerading as a Duke. On the other hand we know, from what the poets or their associates have told us, that Wordsworth's

"Tintern Abbey," Coleridge's "Dejection," Shelley's "Ode to the West Wind," and Keats's "Why Did I Laugh Tonight?" were based on personal experience, and these lyrics may be meaningfully called subjective.

Even poems that are subjective in this fashion, however, carry no warrant of autobiographical accuracy. The poet may ground a poem on his private experiences and feelings, but as a poet he is free—in fact, he is obliged—to invent, alter, and organize his material according to purely poetic rather than autobiographical criteria. Furthermore, the subjectivity of these poems is more the concern of the biographer and literary historian than of the critic. If the subjective poem is a good poem, it is self-sufficient, shaped by its own inner principle, and capable of being fully read without reference to the poet in his own person.

Objective criticism undertakes to analyze and evaluate literary works by the application of universal principles, distinctions, and criteria; **subjective criticism,** which emphasizes rather the feelingful responses evoked by the poem from the critic as an individual, is the equivalent of **impressionistic criticism** (see under **Criticism**).

Occasional poems are written to adorn or memorialize a specific event, such as a birthday, a death, the dedication of a public building, or the opening performance of a play. Milton's "Lycidas," Marvell's "Horatian Ode upon Cromwell's Return from Ireland," and some of Dryden's Prologues and Epilogues written for theatrical productions are instances of poems that have survived their occasions. The English poet laureate is often called on to meet the emergency of royal anniversaries and public events with an appropriate *œuvre.*

Octave. See **Sonnet.**

Octavo. See **Folio.**

Ode. The term "ode" is usually employed for a long lyric poem, serious in subject, elevated in style, and elaborate in its stanzaic structure. As Norman Maclean put it, the word "ode" now calls to mind a lyric which is "massive, public in its proclamations, and Pindaric in its classical prototype" ("From Action to Image," in *Critics and Criticism,* ed. R. S. Crane, 1952). The Greek odes of Pindar, modeled on the choric songs in the drama (see **Chorus**), had stanzas patterned in sets of three: moving to the left, the chorus chanted the **strophe;** moving to the right, the **antistrophe;** then, standing still, the **epode.** The **Pindaric ode** in English is a learned imitation of this form, with the strophes and antistrophes written in one stanza form, and the epodes in another. The construction of the regular Pindaric ode may be conveniently studied in Thomas Gray's "The Progress of Poesy."

The **irregular** or **Cowleyan ode** was introduced in 1656 by Abraham

Cowley, who disregarded the strophic triad and allowed each stanza to find its own pattern of line lengths, number of lines, and rhyme scheme. This freely altering stanza has been the most common for the English ode ever since; Wordsworth's great ode on "Intimations of Immortality" is representative. What the Latin poet, Horace, called "odes" we would now call lyrics and songs. Their influence is found in certain less solemn and formal English odes, often "monostrophic" in form; i.e., written in a single repetitive stanza. Examples are Marvell's "Horatian Ode upon Cromwell's Return from Ireland," and the odes of Keats.

Pindar's odes were **encomiastic,** or written to praise and glorify someone—in this instance, the winners in the Olympic games. The earlier English odes—and many later ones—were also written to eulogize people (Dryden's "Anne Killigrew"), or the arts of music or poetry (Dryden's "Alexander's Feast"), or a natural scene (Collins' "Ode to Evening" and Keats's ode "To Autumn"), or abstract concepts (Gray's "Hymn to Adversity" and Wordsworth's "Ode to Duty"). Romantic poets perfected the ode of passionate meditation, which is stimulated by an aspect of the landscape and turns on the attempt to resolve a personal or generically human problem (Wordsworth's "Intimations Ode," Coleridge's "Dejection"); an interesting recent example of this type is Allen Tate's "Ode to the Confederate Dead." See **Lyric;** and for reference, George N. Shuster, *The English Ode from Milton to Keats* (1940).

Onomatopoeia is the use of words whose sounds seem to resemble the sounds they describe: "hiss," "buzz," "rustle," "bang." There is no exact duplication, however, of the inanimate by the verbal sounds; the apparent similarity is due as much to the meaning as to the physical character of the words. Tennyson exploited the device, in a gamut of effects from

> The moan of doves in immemorial elms,
> And murmur of innumerable bees,

to

>   I heard them blast
> The steep slate-quarry, and the great echo flap,
> And buffet round the hills, from bluff to bluff.

The sounds mimicked need not be pleasant ones. Browning, for one, liked squishy and scratchy effects, as in "Meeting at Night":

> As I gain the cove with pushing prow,
> And quench its speed i' the slushy sand . . . .

> A tap at the pane, the quick sharp scratch
> And blue spurt of a lighted match.

See also **Alliteration** and **Euphony and Cacophony.**

Originality. See **Convention and Tradition.**

Ottava rima. See **Stanza.**

Oxymoron. See **Figurative language.**

Parable. See **Allegory.**

Paradox. See **Figurative language.**

Paranomasia. See **Figurative language.**

Parody. See **Burlesque and Parody.**

Pastoral. A pastoral poem was originally about "pastors," that is, shepherds, but the term has been extended to cover all works that deal with rural life. The originator of the form was Theocritus, a Greek who wrote about Sicilian shepherds in the third century B.C. Virgil later imitated Theocritus in his Latin *Eclogues* and established the enduring model for the pastoral: an elaborately conventional poem expressing an urban poet's nostalgic image of the golden peace and simplicity of a pastoral existence (see **Convention and Tradition**). The conventions which later poets imitated from Virgil's imitations of Theocritus involve a shepherd, reclining under a spreading beech and meditating the rural muse, or engaging in a friendly singing contest, or lamenting his ill-fortune with a beautiful but unresponsive mistress, or grieving over the death of a fellow shepherd. From the classic treatments of this last theme developed an independent form that produced the greatest single pastoral poems and persisted long after other pastoral types had disappeared: see **pastoral elegy** under **Elegy.**

In the Renaissance the pastoral was adapted to satiric and allegorical uses. Spenser's *Shepherd's Calendar* (1579) included almost all the varieties of the pastoral current in this period. Such was the vogue of the form that Renaissance writers applied it to many new literary uses. There was the pastoral romance in prose (Sidney's *Arcadia*), the pastoral lyric (Marlowe's "The Passionate Shepherd to His Love"), and the pastoral drama. Fletcher's *The Faithful Shepherdess* is an example of this last type, and Shakespeare's *As You Like It* centers around the green pastoral world of Arden, where all enmities are reconciled, all problems resolved, and the course of true love made to run smooth.

Other terms sometimes used for the pastoral are **idyll**, from the name given to Theocritus' poems, or **eclogue** (literally, "a selection"), from the title of Virgil's pastorals, or **bucolic poetry**, from the Greek word for "herdsman." The last important collection of Virgilian pastorals, that calculated and graceful exploitation of pure artifice, was Pope's *Pastorals* (1709). Five years later Gay's *Shepherd's Week* burlesqued the type by applying its elegant formulae to actual rustic people and concerns, and inadvertently showed the way to the seriously realistic treatment of rural subjects. (See **Burlesque and Parody.**) In 1783 George Crabbe published *The Village* in order specifically to

> paint the cot
> As Truth will paint it and as bards will not.

How far the term then lost its traditional connotation is indicated by Wordsworth's title for his realistic rendering of a rural tragedy in 1800: "Michael, a Pastoral Poem." See W. W. Greg, *Pastoral Poetry and Pastoral Drama* (1906), and William Empson, *Some Versions of Pastoral* (1935).

Pathetic fallacy was a phrase invented by John Ruskin in 1856 to designate the description of an inanimate object as though it had human capacities and feelings (*Modern Painters,* Vol. III, Part IV). As used by Ruskin the term was derogatory, since it applied, he said, not to the "true appearances of things to us," but to "the extraordinary, or false appearances, when we are under the influence of emotion, or contemplative fancy." Two of his examples are

> The spendthrift crocus, bursting through the mould
> Naked and shivering, with his cup of gold,

and Coleridge's

> The one red leaf, the last of its clan,
> That dances as often as dance it can.

These passages, Ruskin says, however beautiful, are untrue and "morbid"; in the greatest poets, the pathetic fallacy occurs rarely, and only at a point beyond which it would be inhuman to resist the pressure of the feelings to humanize the facts of perception.

Ruskin's criterion, however, would make the greatest poets, including Shakespeare, "morbid." His term is now used, for the most part, as a neutral way to define a very common poetic phenomenon. "The pathetic fallacy" is applied especially to passages in which the attribution of human traits to natural objects is more unobtrusive and less formal than in the figure known as **personification** (see under **Figurative language**).

Pathos and Bathos. Pathos in the Greek means suffering or passion; in criticism it is attributed to a scene or passage designed to evoke tenderness, pity, or sorrow from the audience. At the end of Act IV in *Hamlet,* the queen's speech describing to Laertes the drowning of his sister Ophelia is imbued with pathos; in rendering the death of Little Nell in

The Old Curiosity Shop, Dickens exploits pathos beyond the endurance of most readers today. See **Sensibility and Sentimentalism.**

Bathos is Greek for "depth." It has been an indispensable critical term since Alexander Pope, inspired by Longinus' *On Sublimity* ("loftiness"), wrote in 1727 a mock-critical treatise called *On Bathos, or, Of the Art of Sinking in Poetry.* In this work Pope solemnly assures his readers that he undertakes "to lead them as it were by the hand . . . the gentle down-hill way to Bathos; the bottom, the end, the central point, the *non plus ultra,* of true Modern Poesy!" The word is used for a sudden descent in literature when, straining at the pathetic or sublime, the writer overshoots the mark and tumbles into the ridiculous. Bathos should not be confused with intentional **anticlimax,** which a writer may use for satiric or comic effect. Thus Thomas Gray in his "Ode on the Death of a Favorite Cat," drowned when she stretched too far over a tub of water in trying to catch a goldfish, gravely inserts the observation:

> What female heart can gold despise?
> What cat's averse to fish?

The comic glory of true bathos resides in the author's inadvertently achieving this effect while attempting with all his might to do the opposite. Pope in his examples records what he calls the "modest request of two absent lovers" in a contemporary poem:

> Ye Gods! annihilate but Space and Time,
> And make two lovers happy.

The slogan "For God, for Country, and for Yale" is bathetic because it moves to intentional climax in rhetorical order, and unintentional anticlimax in significance—at least for someone who is not a Yale man. But the author of the slogan can take comfort; the greatest of poets fall unwittingly into the same rhetorical figure. Wordsworth, after relating at length the sad tale of the star-crossed lovers, Vaudracour and Julia, tells how Julia died, leaving Vaudracour to raise their infant son:

> It consoled him here
> To attend upon the orphan, and perform
> Obsequious service to the precious child
> Which, after a short time, by some mistake
> Or indiscretion of the Father, died.

Periodic sentence. See **Style.**

Peripety. See **Plot and Character.**

Periphrasis. See **Diction.**

Personification. See **Figurative language** and **Pathetic fallacy.**

Picaresque story. See **Novel.**

Platonic love. In Plato's *Symposium,* Socrates recounts the advice of the wise woman, Diotima, not to linger over the love of beauty as exhibited by a single individual but to mount up as by a stair, "from one going on to two, and from two to all fair forms," until one arrives at the contemplation of the Idea of "beauty absolute, separate, simple, and everlasting," of which the passing beauties of the world of sense are only a distant and distorted reflection. From this doctrine, and from the writings of later philosophers like Plotinus, Renaissance thinkers developed the theory that physical beauty is only the outer sign of a moral and spiritual beauty of the soul, which is in turn rayed out from the absolute Beauty of God Himself. The Platonic lover, therefore, reverences the physical beauty of the beloved only as a manifestation of spirit, and regards it as the lowest rung in the ladder leading up from sensual desire to the pure contemplation of Heavenly Beauty in God. (See the exposition in Book IV of Castiglione's *The Courtier,* 1528, and in Spenser's "Hymn in Honor of Beauty.") As Spenser wrote in one of the sonnets called *Amoretti:*

> Men call you fayre, and you doe credit it. . . .
> But only that is permanent and free
> From frayle corruption, that doth flesh ensew.
> That is true beautie: that doth argue you
> To be divine and borne of heavenly seed:
> Derived from that fayre Spirit, from whom al true
> And perfect beauty did at first proceed.

From this complex religious and philosophical doctrine, the later concept that Platonic love is love divorced from sexual desire is a vulgarized abstraction.

The concept of Platonic love has fascinated later poets, especially Shelley (see his "Epipsychidion"). But in real life Shelley and other lovers have found that the Platonic ladder is rather slippery, and also that the locus of the Platonic Idea of Beauty tends to move disconcertingly from one earthly woman to another. "Oh Plato! Plato!" Byron sighed,

> you have paved the way,
> With your confounded fantasies, to more
> Immoral conduct by the fancied sway
> Your system feigns o'er the controlless core
> Of human hearts, than all the long array
> Of poets and romancers. . . .

See **Renaissance,** and refer to J. S. Harrison, *Platonism in English Poetry of the Sixteenth and Seventeenth Centuries* (1903), and Paul Shorey, *Platonism Ancient and Modern* (1938).

Plot and Character. The plot is the system of actions represented in a dramatic or narrative work, and the characters are the people, endowed with specific moral and dispositional qualities, who carry on the action. This definition is deceptively simple, because in critical discussions the terms "action" and "character" are given variable and reciprocal significance; that is, either one of these terms can be expanded to take over more and more of the other's area of meaning. "Action" may mean only pantomime—what a deaf man would perceive if he attended a play—or it may be broadened to include also the verbal actions—the **dialogue,** or conversation—carried on by the characters, and to include even the mental action, or the thoughts and feelings of the characters. Conversely, the sphere of "character" can be progressively widened to include the thought and speeches in which it manifests itself, as well as the physical actions which are motivated by a person's character. For example, Aristotle—whose acute commentary in the *Poetics* has been the basis for discussions of dramatic and narrative forms ever since—said that the plot is the "end and purpose," the "life and soul" of tragedy, to which the characters are subordinate. On this account Aristotle has often been charged with justifying only melodrama and sheer action stories. But Aristotle meant by plot, in this context, the *total* actions, in thought, word, and deed, of the specified characters in a play. Aristotle's critics, on the other hand, usually mean by plot an abstract pattern of action largely independent of the specific character of the agents: the summary we give, for example, when someone asks us what a play or novel is about, or that we read in books like *The Hundred Best Novels Condensed*. It is important to remain alert to this sliding boundary between the words "plot" and "character" if we are to read critical commentaries with understanding or to discuss narrative and dramatic forms with intelligence.

There is a great variety of plot forms. For example, some plots are devised to illustrate and enforce a doctrine (see **Allegory** and **Didactic**), while others are elements in works presented for their own aesthetic interest. And in the latter works, some plots are tragic and some are comic, and each of these types in turn exhibits an indefinite variety of plot patterns, represented in both narrative and dramatic forms. No one set of formulae will cover all the varieties of plot that have been embodied in successful works of literature. The following terms, however, widely current in criticism, are useful in discussing the relation of characters to plots, in discriminating types of plots, and in analyzing plots into their component elements.

We require of a character that his **motivation**—the grounds for his actions in his moral nature and personality—be clear and consistent; the character may remain static or he may change, but he ought not suddenly to break off and act in a way not grounded in his temperament as we already know it. We also want a character to be convincing and lifelike. E. M. Forster has introduced popular new terms for an old distinction in discriminating **flat** from **round** characters. A flat character (who used to be called a "type") is presented only in outline without much individualizing detail, and so can readily be described in a single phrase or sentence. A round character is a complex and fully realized individual, and therefore is as difficult to describe with any adequacy as most people are in real life. All plots, properly enough, have many flat characters; there is no need for Mistress Quickly to be as globular as Falstaff. And in many types of plot, such as the detective story or adventure tale or farce comedy, we do not demand that even the leading characters be more than two-dimensional. Sherlock Holmes and Long John Silver do not require, for their own excellent literary functions, the roundness of a Hamlet or a Becky Sharp.

The chief character in a work is called the **protagonist,** or **hero,** and if he is pitted against an important opponent, that character is called an **antagonist.** Hamlet is the protagonist and King Claudius the antagonist in Shakespeare's play, and the relation between them is one of **conflict.** In addition to the conflict between individuals there may be the conflict of a character against the circumstances intervening between him and a goal he has set himself, and the conflict of opposing tendencies within a single individual's mind; an example of this last type is the inner struggle between Hamlet's desire to avenge his father and his propensity to delay. If any one of the characters sets up a scheme which depends for its success on the ignorance of the person or persons against whom it is directed, it is called an **intrigue.** Iago intrigues against Othello and Cassio in Shakespeare's *Othello.* A number of comedies, such as Ben Jonson's *Volpone* and many Restoration plays, have plots which are primarily concerned with the success or failure of an intrigue.

As a plot progresses, it arouses various expectations in the audience or reader about the future course of events. An anxious uncertainty about what is going to happen, especially to those characters with whom we have established bonds of sympathy, is known as **suspense.** If what in fact happens violates the expectations we have formed, it is known as **surprise.** The interplay of suspense and surprise is a prime source of the magnetic power of a plot; but the most effective surprise is that which turns out to have been thoroughly grounded in what has gone before, even though we have hitherto made the wrong inference from the given facts. As E. M. Forster put it, the shock of the unexpected, "followed by the feeling, 'oh, that's all right,' is a sign that all is well with the plot." **Dramatic irony** is that special kind of suspenseful expectation which arises when we foresee the oncoming disaster but the characters do not (see under **Irony**).

A plot has **unity of action** if it is a single, complete, and ordered action, in which none of the parts is unnecessary, and as Aristotle said, all the parts are "so closely connected that the transposal or withdrawal of any one of them will disjoint and dislocate the whole." It follows that for perfect unity all the action included must be **significant action;** events immaterial to the evolution of the plot are omitted. This selection of matter and its organization into a plot pattern distinguish an artistic narrative from the flux of events in real life. Throughout *Macbeth,* for example, it is assumed that the characters spend most nights in sleep. But this action is represented or alluded to only on the occasions when it has significance in the evolution of the plot: on one night when King Duncan slept, Macbeth and Lady Macbeth stayed awake to murder him; and later because of this deed they themselves lost the gift of quiet sleep. Aristotle also pointed out that it does not constitute a unified plot to present a series of episodes which are strung together because they happen to a single subject. Many picaresque novels, nevertheless, such as Defoe's *Moll Flanders,* have held the interest of readers for centuries with this episodic kind of structure (see under **Novel**). One of the later literary developments which Aristotle did not foresee is the kind of unity possible with **double plots,** familiar in Elizabethan drama, in which a subplot is presented in the relation of analogue or counterpoint to the main action. The Gloucester story in *King Lear* and the Falstaff episodes in *Henry IV, Part 1,* are examples of highly successful subplots in Shakespeare.

The order of the unified plot, as Aristotle said, is a continuous sequence of beginning, middle, and end. The beginning initiates the action, the middle presumes what has gone before and requires something to follow, and the end follows from what has gone before but requires nothing further: we are satisfied that the story is complete. The beginning, or "point of attack," need not be the birth of the hero or even the initial stages of the specific events brought to a climax in the story. The epic, for example, plunges *in medias res* (see **Epic**), and the writer of a drama usually begins close to an event that precipitates the central situation or conflict. *Romeo and Juliet* opens with a street fight between servants, and *Hamlet* with the apparition of a ghost; the necessary **exposition** of the backgrounds—the feud between the Capulets and Montagues, or the posture of affairs in the Royal House of Denmark— Shakespeare weaves skillfully into the course of the dialogue and action of these dramatic opening scenes. In the novel, the modern drama, and the motion picture, such exposition is sometimes managed by **flashbacks,** or interpolated descriptions or scenes representing events that happened before the point at which the story opens.

The German critic, Gustav Freytag, in the mid-nineteenth century proposed an analysis of the typical structure of a five-act play as composed of rising action, climax, and falling action; these terms are frequently echoed, even though the total pattern which Freytag described applies only to a limited number of plays. After the opening scene and exposition in *Hamlet*, for example, the **rising action** (or what Aristotle called the **complication**) begins with the ghost telling Hamlet of his murder, and continues with the conflict between Hamlet and Claudius, in which Hamlet, despite setbacks, succeeds in controlling the course of events. The highest point of the rising action, the **climax**, comes with the proof to Hamlet of the king's guilt by the device of the play within the play, Act III, scene ii. The **falling action** begins at the "turning point," or Hamlet's failure to kill the king while he is at prayer. From now on the antagonist, Claudius, for the most part controls the action, until the tragic **catastrophe**, at which point occurs the death of the hero, as well as of Claudius, his Queen, and Laertes. A more general term for this point of a play and what follows, which applies to comedy as well as tragedy, is the **denouement**, or "unknotting" of the plot: the action or intrigue ends in success or failure, or the mystery is solved, or the misunderstanding is cleared away. The denouement sometimes involves a **discovery**, or disclosure of an important fact hitherto unknown to a principal character; thus Caesario reveals himself to be Viola at the end of *Twelfth Night*, or the fact of Iago's treachery finally becomes clear to Othello. The denouement often includes also a **peripety**, or **reversal**, in the hero's fortunes, whether to his destruction, as in Shakespearean tragedy, or to his success, as in *Tom Jones* and many other comic plots.

In some Greek tragedies the complication of the plot is resolved by a **deus ex machina**, or a god lowered in a stage machine, who merely commands the desired result and so extricates the hero from his difficulty. The phrase is now used for any forced and improbable device with which a hard-pressed author makes shift to resolve his plot.

In the sixteenth and seventeenth centuries, neoclassic critics of the drama in Italy and France added to Aristotle's requirement for unity of action two others, to make up what were called the **three unities**. On the assumption that the action represented in a play should approximate the actual conditions of the stage production, they required "unity of place" (that the represented action be limited to one location) and "unity of time" (that the time represented as passing be no more than one day). A famous attack on the unities of time and place will be found in Dr. Johnson's "Preface to Shakespeare" (1765). Since the mid-eighteenth century in England the unities of time and place have been regarded as optional devices, available to the dramatist for special effects of dramatic concentration.

For related topics see **Comedy, Novel, Short story, Tragedy.**

Poetic diction. See **Diction.**

Poetic Justice. See **Tragedy.**

Poetic license. Dryden defined poetic license as "the liberty which poets have assumed to themselves, in all ages, of speaking things in verse, which are beyond the severity of prose." In the narrow sense the term is applied to diction alone, to justify the poet's departure from standard prose in the choice, order, or pronunciation of words. In a wider sense the term has been applied to the poet's use of fiction, myth, meter, rhyme—to all the ways, that is, in which poetry, for its own ends, departs from fact and the ordinary use of language. The degree and kinds of "license" allowed to poets have varied according to the conventions and sensibilities of each age, but in every case the justification of the freedom lies in the success of the effect (see **Convention and Tradition**). The great opening sentence of Milton's *Paradise Lost* violates the conventions of standard English prose in word order, word choice, figurative construction, even grammar, in order to achieve the grandeur of announcement commensurate with the dimensions of his epic subject and form. Nor need it diminish our delight in the poetic product that Shakespeare dressed his Cleopatra in corsets and assumed that Bohemia had a seacoast, or that Keats, in "On First Looking into Chapman's Homer," ignorantly made Cortez instead of Balboa the discoverer of the Pacific Ocean.

Point of view refers to the outlook from which the events in a novel or short story are related. There are many variations and combinations of points of view, but the principal modes are (1) The author tells the story omnisciently, moving from character to character and event to event, having free access to the motivation, thoughts, and feelings of his characters, and introducing information to the reader when and where he chooses. In a number of novels so constructed, such as Fielding's *Tom Jones* and Thackeray's *Vanity Fair,* the novelist does not tell the tale impersonally but acts as a commentator on the characters and their actions. (2) The author narrates the story in the third person, but chooses one character as his "sentient center" whom he follows throughout the action, restricting the reader to the field of vision and range of knowledge of that character alone (Henry James's *The Ambassadors*). (3) The story is told in the first person by one of the characters himself, who may be the protagonist (Dickens' *David Copperfield*) or only a minor observer of the action (Emily Brontë's *Wuthering Heights*). John Dos Passos' *USA*, Virgina Woolf's *Mrs. Dalloway,* and James Joyce's *Ulysses* and *Finnegans Wake* give some notion of the directions and vigor of the experimentation with point of view in modern fiction. See **Novel.**

Portmanteau word. See **Ambiguity.**

Primitivism. A primitivist is someone who opposes "nature" (in the sense of what exists independently of man's contrivance) to "art" (or what man accomplishes by work, thought, and inherited laws and conventions), and gives his allegiance to "nature." **Cultural primitivism,** as this preference of nature over art has been called, can be exhibited in any field of values. For example, in social philosophy a primitivist prefers simple and "natural" forms of social and political organization to more highly developed and elaborate forms; in ethics, he lauds the "natural" instincts and passions over reason and forethought; in milieu, he prefers outdoor "nature," untouched by human hands, to cities or gardens; and in literature and the other arts, he puts his reliance on spontaneity and the free play of genius, as against the purposeful adaptation of means to foreseen ends and the reliance on "artificial" forms, rules, and conventions. (Note the primitivistic elements in Wordsworth's poetic theory: see under **Diction** and **Neoclassic and Romantic.**)

The cultural primitivist usually finds, in the modern world, that the life and products of "primitive" peoples, relatively isolated from civilization, are preferable to the life and products of people living in highly civilized countries, and especially in cities. The cult of "the Noble Savage" in English and American literature, and the eighteenth-century vogue for "peasant poetry," were both aspects of primitivism. A cultural primitivist is often a **chronological primitivist** as well, holding that, on the whole, the life and activities of man were much more admirable at an early and "natural" stage of history than at present. The contrary of chronological primitivism is the belief in **progress:** the doctrine that, at least in many important ways, by virtue of the development of man's arts, skills, and wisdom, the course of history exhibits improvement over the centuries.

Primitivism, the nostalgia for natural simplicity over artificial complication, is as old as man's recorded thought, but it had a special vogue among eighteenth-century thinkers, in a movement in which Rousseau was a central figure. Two recent ill-assorted primitivists were D. H. Lawrence, the English novelist and amateur sociologist, and Alfred Rosenberg, official philosopher of the Nazi movement, who sounded the call for a return to the supposedly primitive Germanic virtues of blood, soil, and obedience. But most of us are primitivists in some moods, longing to get away from the fret and anxiety of civilization to the supposed simplicities of the natural life. See A. O. Lovejoy and George Boas, *Primitivism and Related Ideas in Antiquity* (1935); A. O. Lovejoy, *Essays in the History of Ideas* (1948); J. B. Bury, *The Idea of Progress* (1932).

Problem play. See **Tragedy.**

Progress, The Idea of. See **Primitivism.**

Propaganda. See **Didactic.**

Prosody. The term "prosody" is used for the systematic study of versification, including meter, rhyme, and stanza forms. See **Meter, Rhyme, Stanza.**

Prosopopoeia. See **Figurative language.**

Protagonist. See **Plot and Character.**

Pun. See **Figurative language.**

Puritan Period. See **Commonwealth Period.**

Purple passage is a sudden heightening of style, in rhythm, diction, and use of figures, which makes a section of prose or verse stand out from its context (see **Style**). The term is sometimes applied without derogation to a set piece, separable and quotable, in which an author rises to an occasion. Examples are the famous speech on England by the dying John of Gaunt in Shakespeare's *Richard II*, beginning

> This royal throne of kings, this scepter'd isle,
> This earth of majesty, this seat of Mars—

and Byron's description of the Duchess of Richmond's ball in *Childe Harold*, Canto III. Often, however, the term connotes a sneer at an author who has self-consciously girded himself to perform a piece of fine writing.

Quarto. See **Folio.**

Quatrain. See **Stanza.**

Realism and Naturalism. "Realistic fiction" is often opposed to "romantic fiction." The romance is said to present life as we would have it be, more picturesque, more adventurous, more heroic than the actual; realism, to present an accurate picture of life as it is. This distinction is inadequate. Casanova, T. E. Lawrence, Winston Churchill are all people in real life, but their histories, as related by themselves or others, demonstrate that truth is stranger than realism. The realistic writer prefers as protagonist an ordinary citizen of Middletown, living on Main Street, perhaps, and engaged in the real estate business. The realist, in other words, is deliberately selective in his material and prefers the commonplace and everyday over the rarer aspects of the contemporary scene. His characters are usually of the middle class or working class; people without exceptional endowments, who live through ordinary experiences of childhood, adolescence, love, marriage, parenthood, and infidelity; who find life rather unhappy and dull, though it may be brightened by touches of joy and beauty; but who may, under special circumstances, display something akin to heroism.

A thoroughgoing realism involves not only a selection of subject matter but, more importantly, a special literary manner as well: the subject is presented, or "rendered," in a certain way. The first novelistic realist, Daniel Defoe, dealt with the extraordinary adventures of a shipwrecked mariner named Robinson Crusoe and with the extraordinary misadventures of Moll Flanders, who was born in jail, "twelve year a whore, five times a Wife (whereof once to her own brother)," and so on. But these novels are made to seem the very mirror held up to real life by Defoe's reportorial manner of rendering the events, whether trivial or extraordinary, in the same circumstantial, matter-of-fact, and seemingly unselective way. Writers such as Henry Fielding and Jane Austen are sometimes called realists because they often render commonplace people so well that they convince us such people really lived and talked this way. It is better, however, to save the term "realist" for writers who on the whole render a subject seriously, and as though it were a direct reflection of life, without obviously shaping it, as do Fielding and Austen, into a basically comic or ironic pattern. It makes good sense to say that Jane Austen is *more* realistic in subject and manner than the contemporary writer of romances, Sir Walter Scott; or that Jane Austen's novels contain many realistic passages. The technical term, "realistic novel," however, is most usefully applied to works which are realistic both in subject and manner, and throughout the whole, rather than in parts—works such as William Dean Howells' *The Rise of Silas Lapham*, Arnold Bennett's novels about the "Five Towns," and Sinclair Lewis' *Main Street*.

Naturalism is sometimes claimed to be an even more accurate picture of life than is realism. But naturalism is not only, like realism, a special selection of subject matter and a special literary manner; it is a mode of fiction which was developed in accordance with a special philosophical thesis. This thesis, a product of post-Darwinian biology in the mid-nineteenth century, held that man belongs entirely in the order of nature and does not have a soul or any other connection with a religious or spiritual world beyond nature; that man is therefore merely a higher-order animal whose character and fortunes are determined by two kinds of natural forces, heredity and environment. He inherits his personal traits and his compulsive instincts, especially hunger and sex, and he is subject to the economic and social forces in the environment into which he is born. Accordingly, the French novelist Émile Zola, who did much to develop this theory, and later writers such as the Americans, Theodore Dreiser and James Farrell, try to present their subjects with an objective scientific attitude and with elaborate documentation, including an almost medical frankness about activities and bodily functions usually unmentioned in earlier literature. They often choose characters who exhibit strong animal drives, such as greed and brutal sexual desire, and who are helplessly subject both to their glandular secretions within and to sociological pressures without. The end of the naturalistic novel is usually "tragic," but not, as in classical and Elizabethan tragedy, because of a heroic but losing struggle of the individual mind and will against gods, enemies, and circumstance. The protagonist of the naturalistic story, a pawn to multiple compulsions, merely disintegrates or is wiped out (see **Tragedy**). Aspects of naturalistic subject and manner are apparent in major modern writers of the novel and drama such as Thomas Hardy, James Joyce, and Eugene O'Neill; and it will be obvious how much a modern tragedy such as Arthur Miller's *Death of a Salesman* owes to this movement. An enlightening exercise is to distinguish how love, or the relation between the sexes, is treated in a romantic novel (Richard Blackmore's *Lorna Doone*), a realistic novel (William Dean Howells' *A Modern Instance*), and a naturalistic novel (Émile Zola's *Nana*, or Theodore Dreiser's *An American Tragedy*). See **Novel;** and for movements originally opposed to realism and naturalism (though some modern works, such as Joyce's *Ulysses*, combine all these techniques), see **Expressionism**, and **symbolism** (under **Symbol**).

Naturalism is sometimes used, in a totally different sense, to apply to writers, such as Wordsworth and Robert Frost, who deal in loving detail with "nature," or the outdoor scene.

Reformation. See **Renaissance.**

Refrain. See **Stanza.**

Renaissance means "rebirth," and is the name applied to the historical period following the Middle Ages. The Renaissance is usually said to have begun in Italy in the late fourteenth century and to have continued through the fifteenth and sixteenth centuries. In this period in Western Europe the arts of painting, sculpture, architecture, and literature reached an eminence not exceeded by any civilization in any age. The development came late to England, in the sixteenth century, and did not have its flowering time until the Elizabethan and Jacobean periods (see **Elizabethan Age** and **Jacobean Age**); sometimes, in fact, Milton (1608–1674) is said to be the last great Renaissance poet.

Many attempts have been made to define "the spirit of the Renaissance," as though one essence underlay the complex attributes of the civilization of numerous countries over several hundred years. It has been described as the birth of the modern world out of the ashes of the dark ages; as the discovery of the world and the discovery of man; as the era of untrammelled individualism in life, thought, religion, and art. Recently some historians, finding these Renaissance characteristics in various people and places in the Middle Ages, and finding also that many elements long held to be medieval survived into the Renaissance, have denied that the Renaissance ever existed. It is true that history is a continuous process, and that "periods" are invented not by God but by historians; but the concept of a period is a convenience, if not a necessity, of historical analysis, and one is certainly able to identify, during the span of the Renaissance, a number of events and discoveries which in the course of time altered radically the views, productions, and manner of life of European men.

All these events may be regarded as putting a strain on the relatively closed and stable world of the great civilization of the later Middle Ages, when most of the really essential truths about man, the universe, religion, and philosophy were held to be fairly well known and permanently established. The full impact of many of these Renaissance discoveries did not make itself felt until the later seventeenth and the eighteenth centuries, but the very fact that they occurred in this period indicates the vitality, the boldness, and the restless curiosity of many men of the Renaissance, whether scholars, thinkers, artists, or adventurers.

1. The new learning. Renaissance scholars of the classics, called "humanists," revived the knowledge of the Greek language, discovered and disseminated a great number of Greek manuscripts, and added considerably to the number of Roman authors and works which had been known to the Middle Ages (see **Humanism**). The result was to enlarge immensely the stock of ideas, materials, styles, and literary forms available to Renaissance writers. In the mid-fifteenth century the invention of printing on paper from moveable type made books for the first time cheap and plentiful, and floods of publications, ancient and modern, in the original languages and in translation, poured from the presses of Europe to satisfy the demands of the rapidly expanding literate audience. The speed of the inauguration and spread of ideas, discoveries, and literary forms in the Renaissance was made possible by this technological development.

The humanistic revival sometimes resulted in pedantic scholarship, sterile imitations of ancient works and styles, and a fixed and rigid rhetoric and literary criticism. It also bred, however, the gracious and tolerant humanity of an Erasmus, and the noble concept of the cultivated

Renaissance gentleman expressed in Baldassare Castiglione's *Il Cortegiano* (*The Courtier*), published in 1528. This book was the most admired, translated, and widely read of the many Renaissance **courtesy books,** or books on the nature, obligations, and training of the man of the court. It presents the ideal of the completely rounded or "universal" man, developed in all his faculties and skills, physical, intellectual, and artistic; trained to be a warrior and statesman, but capable also as athlete, philosopher, artist, conversationist, and man of society; whose relations to women are governed by the complex quasi-religious code of Platonic love (see **Platonic love**), and whose actions are crowned by the grace of *sprezzatura*—the seeming ease and negligence with which he conforms to a complex and exacting pattern of behavior. Leonardo da Vinci in Italy and Sir Philip Sidney in England were living embodiments of this ideal.

2. The new religion. The **Reformation** led by Martin Luther (1483–1546) was a successful heresy which struck at the very basis of the institutionalism of the Roman Catholic Church. This early Protestantism was grounded on the individual's inner experience of spiritual struggle and salvation. Faith (based on the word of the Bible as interpreted by the individual) was alone thought competent to save, and salvation itself was regarded as a direct transaction with God in the theater of the individual soul, without need or possibility of intermediation by Church, priest, or sacrament. For this reason Protestantism is sometimes said to have been the extreme manifestation of "Renaissance individualism," although it soon developed its own institutionalism in the theocracy proposed by John Calvin and his Puritan followers. England in characteristic fashion muddled its way into Protestantism under Henry VIII and Elizabeth, empirically finding a middle way that minimized violence and hastened a stable settlement.

3. The new world. In 1492 Columbus, acting on a revival of the old Greek idea that the world is a globe, sailed West to find a new commercial route to the East, only to be frustrated by the unexpected barrier of a new continent. The succeeding explorations of this continent gave new materials and stimulus to the literary imagination. More important for literature, however, was the fact that economic exploitation of the new world put England at the center, rather than as heretofore at the edge of the trade routes, and so helped establish the commercial prosperity that in England, as in Italy earlier, was a necessary though not sufficient condition for the development of a vigorous intellectual and artistic life.

4. The new cosmos. The cosmos of medieval astronomy and theology was the Ptolemaic one, picturing a stationary earth around which rotated the successive spheres of the moon, the various planets, and the fixed stars; Heaven, or the Empyrean, was often thought to be situ-

ated above the spheres, and Hell either below the spheres or at the center of the Earth. In 1543 Copernicus published his new hypothesis concerning the structure of the universe, which undertook to give a simpler and more consistent explanation of the accumulated observations of the movements of the heavenly bodies. The Copernican theory pictured the cosmos as a system in which the center is not the earth, but the sun, and in which the earth is not stationary, but one planet among the many planets which revolve around the sun.

Investigation of the evidence has not borne out the earlier assumption that the world-picture of Copernicus and his followers delivered an immediate and profound shock to the theological and secular beliefs of all thinking men. For example in 1611, when Donne wrote in "The First Anniversary" that "new Philosophy calls all in doubt," for "the Sun is lost, and th' earth," he did so only to support the ancient theme of the world's decay and to enforce a standard Christian *contemptus mundi*. Still later Milton in *Paradise Lost* expressed a suspension of judgment between the Ptolemaic and Copernican theories and adopted for his own poem the older Ptolemaic scheme because it was more firmly traditional and better adapted to his imaginative purposes. Much more important, in the long run, was the effect on men's opinions of the general principles and methods of the "new science" of the great successors of Copernicus such as Kepler and Galileo. The cosmos of many Elizabethan writers was not only Ptolemaic, and subject throughout to God's Providence; it was also an animate universe, invested with occult powers, inhabited by daemons and spirits, often thought to control men's lives by stellar influences, and to be itself subject to control by the power of witchcraft and of magic. The cosmos that emerged in the seventeenth century, as a product of the scientific procedure of constructing mathematical hypotheses capable of being tested by precisely measured observations, was the physical universe of René Descartes (1596–1650). "Give me extension and motion," Descartes wrote, "and I will construct the universe." This universe consisted of extended particles of matter which moved in space according to fixed mathematical laws, entirely free from interference by angels, daemons, human prayer, or occult magical powers, and subject only to the limited manipulations of scientists who, in Francis Bacon's phrase, had learned to obey nature in order to be her master. In this way the working hypotheses of the physical scientist were converted into a philosophical world view, which was made current by many popular expositions, and—together with the methodological principle that controlled observation, rather than tradition or authority, is the only test of truth in all areas of knowledge—entered into that part of the climate of eighteenth-century opinion known as the **Enlightenment**.

Refer to J. Burckhardt, *Civilization of the Renaissance in Italy* (first published in 1860); E. A. Burtt, *The Metaphysical Foundations of Modern Science* (1932); C. S. Lewis, *English Literature in the 16th Century* (1954); Marjorie Nicolson, *Science and Imagination* (1956); H. O. Taylor, *Thought and Expression in the 16th Century* (1920).

Repartee. See **Wit and Humor.**

Restoration Period. The period takes its name from the restoration of the Stuart line (Charles II) to the English throne in 1660, at the end of the Commonwealth (see **Commonwealth Period**); it is usually regarded as lasting until the end of the seventeenth century. The urbanity, wit, and licentiousness of the life centering on the court, in reaction to the sobriety and restraint of the earlier Puritan regime, is reflected in much of the literature of this age. The theaters came back to vigorous life after the revocation of the ban placed upon them by the Puritans, and Dryden, Etherege, Wycherley, Otway, Congreve, and other playwrights produced the distinctive type of **Restoration comedy** (see **Comedy**), as well as the serious heroic drama (see **heroic drama** under **Tragedy**). Dryden was the major writer in both verse and prose. Other poets of the time were Samuel Butler and the Earl of Rochester, and other prose writers, Samuel Pepys and Sir William Temple. See also **Neoclassic and Romantic** and **Satire.**

Rhetorical figures. It is convenient to list under the heading "rhetorical figures" certain common figures which depart from the ordinary, or "literal," standard of language mainly by the arrangement of their words to achieve special effects, and not, like metaphors and other "tropes," by a radical change of meaning in the words themselves (see **Figurative language**).

An **apostrophe** is a sudden shift to direct address, either to an absent person or to an abstract or inanimate entity. In the course of his fine poem, "Recollections of Love," Coleridge turns from thoughts of his beloved to apostrophize the River Greta:

> But when those meek eyes first did seem
> To tell me, Love within you wrought—
> O Greta, dear domestic stream!
>
> Has not, since then, Love's prompture deep,
> Has not Love's whisper evermore
> Been ceaseless, as thy gentle roar?
> Sole voice, when other voices sleep,
> Dear under-song in clamor's hour.

If this address is to a god or muse to assist the poet in his composition, it is called an **invocation;** so Milton invokes his muse in *Paradise Lost:*

> And chiefly Thou, O Spirit, that dost prefer
> Before all temples the upright heart and pure,
> Instruct me . . . .

A **rhetorical question** is a question asked, not to evoke a reply, but to achieve a rhetorical emphasis stronger than a direct statement. The figure is most used in persuasive discourse, and tends to impart an oratorical tone to a speech. When "fierce Thalestris" in Pope's *Rape of the Lock* asks Belinda,

> Gods! shall the ravisher display your hair,
> While the fops envy, and the ladies stare?

she does not stay for an answer, which is obviously "No!" (The usual rhetorical question might in fact be described as a question that won't take "Yes" for an answer.) Shelley's "Ode to the West Wind" closes with the most famous rhetorical question in English:

> O, Wind,
> If Winter comes, can Spring be far behind?

Chiasmus is the use of phrases which are syntactically parallel but with their elements reversed, as in this line from Pope, in which the verb first precedes, and then follows, the adverbial phrase:

> *Works* without show, and without pomp *presides.*

The effect is sometimes reinforced by alliteration and other kinds of duplicated sounds; here is Pope's summary of the common fate of coquettes:

> A *fop* their *p*assion, but their *p*rize a *sot.*

Zeugma in Greek means "yoking" and applies to the use of a single word standing in the same grammatical relation to two other terms, but with some alteration in its meaning. So Pope's:

> Or *stain* her honour, or her new brocade.

> *Obliged* by hunger, and request of friends.

> To rest, the cushion and soft Dean *invite.*

To achieve the maximum effects within the tight limits of the closed couplet (see under **Couplet**) Pope exploited all these language patterns with dazzling virtuosity. He is as much the English master of the rhetorical figures as Shakespeare is of the metaphoric figures.

Other rhetorical constructions and sound patterns, defined elsewhere, which are sometimes included under the heading of figures, are **Alliteration, Allusion, antithesis** (under **Couplet**), **Onomatopoeia, periphrasis** (under **Diction**), **Rhyme.**

Rhetorical question. See **Rhetorical figures.**

Rhyme consists in the identity, in the rhyming words, of the last accented vowel and of all the speech sounds following that vowel. If the rhyme includes an unaccented syllable following the accented syllable, it is called a **feminine rhyme;** otherwise it is called a **masculine rhyme.** Here is the last stanza of Wordsworth's "The Solitary Reaper."

> Whate'er the theme, the maiden sang
> As if her song could have no *ending;*
> I saw her singing at her work,
> And o'er the sickle *bending;*—
> I listened, motionless and *still;*
> And, as I mounted up the *hill,*
> The music in my heart I *bore,*
> Long after it was heard no *more.*

The stanza ends with two couplets of masculine rhymes: still-hill, bore–more; lines two and four have a feminine rhyme: ending–bending. A feminine rhyme of two syllables, such as this one, is also called a **double rhyme;** if it consists of three syllables, it is called a **triple rhyme.** Triple rhymes, since they coincide with such surprising patness, often have a humorous quality, as in Byron's description of the hero's mother in *Don Juan:*

> Oh! she was perfect past all parallel—
> Of any modern female saint's *comparison;*
> So far above the cunning powers of hell,
> Her guardian angel had given up his *garrison.*

The comic effect is intensified if the pressure of the rhyme enforces a distortion of pronunciation; so, Byron addresses the husbands of learned ladies:

> But—Oh! ye lords of ladies *intellectual,*
> Inform us truly, have they not hen-*pecked you all?*

This maltreatment of words, in which the poet seems to surrender helplessly to the exigencies of the rhyme, has been thoroughly exploited by Ogden Nash:

> Farewell, farewell, you old rhinoceros,
> I'll stare at something less prepoceros![1]

All the rhymes exemplified so far, coming at the ends of the lines, are called **end rhymes.** Rhymes which occur within a single line, as in the first and third verses of this stanza from Coleridge's "The Ancient Mariner," are called **internal rhymes:**

[1] From *Many Long Years Ago* by Ogden Nash. Copyright, 1933, by Ogden Nash.

> In mist or *cloud,* on mast or *shroud,*
> It perched for vespers nine;
> Whiles all the *night,* through fog-smoke *white,*
> Glimmered the white moon-shine.

If the equivalence of the rhymed sound is exact, it is called **perfect rhyme.** English poets have for the most part used perfect rhymes, except for the liberty of so-called "eye-rhymes," or words whose endings are spelled alike, and in most instances were once pronounced alike, but now have a different pronunciation; for example, prove–love, daughter–laughter (see **Poetic license**). Many modern poets, however, deliberately employ what used to be called **imperfect rhyme,** and is now also called **partial,** or **approximate,** or **slant rhyme.** As early as the latter eighteenth century Blake experimented with such effects, in which the rhymed vowels differ, and occasionally even the consonants are similar rather than identical. Here is a stanza from Wilfred Owen, constructed with two sets of slant rhymes:

> The centuries will burn rich loads
> With which we groaned,
> Whose warmth shall lull their dreamy lids,
> While songs are crooned.
> But they will not dream of us poor lads
> Lost in the ground.[1]

The passages quoted will illustrate some of the many effects of rhyme—the delight given by the expected but variable end chime, the reinforcement of syntax and emphasis when a strong masculine rhyme concurs with the end of a clause or sentence, the grace of movement lent by a feminine rhyme, the broadening of the comic by a pat coincidence of sound or an enforced mispronunciation. Cunning artificers in rhyme make it more than a pleasant sound effect; they use it to enhance or contribute to the meaning. When Pope satirized two contemporary pedants in the lines,

> Yet ne'er one sprig of laurel graced these ribalds,
> From slashing Bentley down to piddling Tibalds,

the rhyme, as W. K. Wimsatt has said, demonstrates "what it means to have a name like that," with its implication that the scholar is as graceless as his appellation. And in one of its most important functions, rhyme binds separate lines into the pattern of a stanza; see **Stanza**.

Rime royal. See **Stanza**.

Rising action. See **Plot and Character**.

Romance. See **Novel** and **Realism and Naturalism**.

Romantic Period. The limits of the Romantic Period are usually set at 1798, the year of publication of Wordsworth's and Coleridge's *Lyrical Ballads,* and 1832, when Scott died and the passage of the Reform Bill signalized the political preoccupations of the Victorian era. For some characteristics of the thought and writings of this great literary period, see **Neoclassic and Romantic.** Other prominent writers of the time were Byron, Shelley, Keats, Lamb, Hazlitt, Landor, and De Quincey.

Rondeau. See **Stanza** and **Vers de société.**

Rules. See **Neoclassic and Romantic.**

Run-on line. See **Meter.**

Sarcasm. See **Irony.**

Satire is the literary art of diminishing a subject by making it ridiculous and evoking towards it attitudes of amusement, contempt, or scorn. It differs from comedy in that comedy evokes laughter as an end in itself, while satire "derides"; that is, it uses laughter as a weapon, and against a butt existing outside the work itself. That butt may be an individual (in "personal satire"), or a type of person, a class, a nation, or even (as in Rochester's "A Satyr against Mankind" and Swift's *Gulliver's Travels*) the whole race of man. (See **Comedy** and **Wit and Humor.**) The distinction between the **comic** and the satiric, however, is a sharp one only at its extremes. Shakespeare's Falstaff is a purely comic creation; his puritanical Malvolio is for the most part comic but has aspects of satire directed against a human type; Jonson's Volpone clearly satirizes the type of man whose cleverness is put at the service of his cupidity; and Dryden's MacFlecknoe, while representing a permanent type of the pretentious poetaster, ridicules specifically the living individual, Shadwell.

Satire has usually been justified by those who practice it as a corrective of human vice and folly. As such, its claim has been to ridicule the failing rather than the individual, and to limit its ridicule to corrigible faults, excluding those for which a man is not responsible. As Swift said, speaking of himself in his "Verses on the Death of Dr. Swift":

> Yet malice never was his aim;
> He lashed the vice, but spared the name. . . .
> His satire points at no defect,
> But what all mortals may correct. . . .
> He spared a hump, or crooked nose,
> Whose owners set not up for beaux.

Satire is frequently found as an incidental element in many works whose over-all form is not satiric, in a certain character, or situation, or passing reference. But in many great literary achievements satire—the attempt to diminish a subject by ridicule—is the organizing principle of the whole. In discussing such writings the following distinctions will be found useful.

One common way of classifying satire is according to its aim and tone (see **Tone**), the two classes taking their names from their great Roman practitioners, Horace and Juvenal. **Horatian satire** undertakes to evoke a smile at the foibles of men; the writer speaks in the character of an urbane and tolerant man of the world who is moved to amusement rather than indignation at the spectacle of human folly—sometimes including his own. **Juvenalian satire** evokes contempt and moral indignation at the vices and corruptions of men; the satirist speaks in the character of a serious moralist denouncing aberrations which are no less dangerous because they are ridiculous. Pope's *Moral Essays* and most of his other writings are Horatian satires; Johnson's "London" and "The Vanity of Human Wishes" are Juvenalian satires.

Another system of classification distinguishes types of satire by their vehicle or form of presentation. **Formal,** or **direct, satire** is a commentary on people and affairs in which the satiric voice speaks out in the first person. Addison writes formal satire in some of his prose essays, and Pope in the verse essay (*Moral Essays*), the epistle ("To Augustus"), or the dialogue ("Epistle to Dr. Arbuthnot"). **Indirect satire** is cast in the form of a plot, in which the characters make themselves ridiculous by their thought, speech, and actions, and are sometimes made even more ridiculous by the author's narrative style and commentary. The articles on **Burlesque and Parody, mock epic** (under **Epic**), **Irony,** and **Wit and Humor** describe some of the many forms and stylistic devices available to indirect satire. Any narrative or dramatic vehicle can be adapted to the purposes of indirect satire. Dryden's *Absalom and Achitophel* turns Old Testament history into a satiric allegory on contemporary political maneuverings. In *Gulliver's Travels* Swift adapts to satiric uses the current narrative of travel. Byron's *Don Juan* is a versified form of the old episodic picaresque story (see **Novel**), and Evelyn Waugh's *The Loved One* is a satiric mode of the prose novel. Ben Jonson and Bernard Shaw wrote satiric comedies for the stage, and Gilbert and Sullivan's *Patience,* like John Gay's *Beggar's Opera* and its modern adaptation, *The Three-penny Opera,* are satiric operettas.

The proportioning of the examples in this article will indicate how large the Restoration and eighteenth century looms in English satiric achievement. Good satire has been written in every period beginning with the Middle Ages, and *Punch* and the *New Yorker* demonstrate that skillful satire still commands a wide audience. But the greatest age of English satire—perhaps of world satire—was the century and a half that included Dryden, Samuel Butler, Addison, Pope, Swift, Gay, Fielding, Johnson, Goldsmith, and (it should not be forgotten in this context)

Burns and Blake. Consult Hugh Walker, *English Satire and Satirists* (1925), and David Worcester, *The Art of Satire* (1940).

Scansion. See **Meter.**

Scene. See **Act.**

Sensibility and Sentimentalism. When a modern critic talks of Donne's "sensibility," or of the "dissociation of sensibility" that set in, according to T. S. Eliot, with the poetry of Milton and Dryden, he seems to mean by the term a person's characteristic emotional and intellectual responsiveness to literature, or to the experience he, as a poet, converts into literature. (See T. S. Eliot, "The Metaphysical Poets," *Selected Essays,* 1932.) When a literary historian, however, talks of "the cult of sensibility" or of "the literature of sensibility," he refers to a particular cultural phenomenon of the eighteenth century. The philosophical background of this tendency was the moral theory that developed as a reaction against seventeenth-century Stoicism, which emphasized reason and the unemotional will as the motive to virtue, and even more importantly, as a reaction against Thomas Hobbes's theory that man is innately selfish, and that the springs of his behavior are self-interest and the drive to power. Sermons, essays, fiction, and philosophical writings (especially the Earl of Shaftesbury's *Characteristicks,* 1711), proclaimed that benevolence, or wishing others well, is innate in man; that virtue is mainly spontaneous action in response to this natural emotion; and that the most important ethical experience is that of sympathy and fellow feeling, or a hair-trigger responsiveness to the joys and distresses of other people. It became a commonplace in popular morality that the ability to shed a sympathetic tear is the sign both of polite breeding and of a virtuous heart. Sensibility thus became **sentimentalism:** an excessive and self-conscious indulgence in the tender emotions of pity and sympathy; or, in the eighteenth-century phrases, a propensity to "the luxury of grief" and "the sadly pleasing tear."

In literature this tendency was reflected especially in the **sentimental comedy,** or **drama of sensibility,** that replaced Restoration comedy (see **Comedy**). In this form, as Goldsmith said, "the virtues of private life are exhibited, rather than the vices exposed, and the distresses rather than the faults of mankind make our interest in the piece"; with the result, he added, that the audience "sit at a play as gloomy as at the tabernacle." The **sentimental novel** similarly emphasized the distresses of the virtuous, either at their own sorrows or at those of their friends (see **Novel**). Laurence Sterne, in *Tristram Shandy* and *A Sentimental Journey,* gives us his own inimitable compound of sensibility and irony. Henry Mackenzie's *The Man of Feeling* (1771) presented a hero of such exquisite sensibility that he went into a decline from an excess of tenderness for a young lady, and died in the perturbation of declaring his emotion. "If his tears had been tears of blood," one critic has said, "the poor man could not have been more debile." Sensibility gave way to solider materials in the nineteenth-century novel, but the mode is still discernible in Dickens' depiction of the death of Little Nell, and Harriet Beecher Stowe's of the death of little Eva. Compare **Pathos and Bathos,** and consult Ernest Bernbaum, *The Drama of Sensibility* (1915); C. A. Moore, *Backgrounds of English Literature, 1700–1760* (1953); and R. P. Utter and G. B. Needham, *Pamela's Daughters* (1936).

Sestet. See **Sonnet.**

Setting. The setting of a narrative or drama is the locale and period in which the action takes place. The setting of *Macbeth,* for example, is medieval Scotland, and that of Joyce's *Ulysses* is Dublin on June 16, 1904. In another sense of the word the setting, or **décor,** of a play consists of the scenery, properties, and costumes used in its staging. See also **regional novel** and **local color** (under **Novel**).

Short story. A short story is a work of prose fiction, and most of the terms and distinctions dealt with in the articles on the novel and other story forms are adaptable to the discussion of the short story as well. It differs, for example, from the **anecdote,** or simple and unelaborated narration of an incident, by organizing characters and their thought, actions, and interactions into the artificial pattern of a plot, which has a beginning, middle, and end, moves to some sort of climax and denouement, and evokes expectation, suspense, and surprise from the reader (see **Novel** and **Plot and Character**). The plot may be comic or tragic, in the many varieties of each of these kinds, and may be in the mode of romance, realism, or naturalism (see **Comedy, Realism and Naturalism, Tragedy**). The focus of interest in the story may be on the course of events, as in Poe's *The Gold Bug* and other tales of detection, and in the often well-contrived but stock narratives of the "pulp" magazines; or it may be on the exhibition of character, as in Katherine Mansfield's stories, in which nothing more may happen than an encounter and conversation between two people. In some stories the interest is balanced between character and action. Hemingway's beautifully managed "The Short Happy Life of Francis Macomber" is as violent in its events as the most lurid adventure tale, but the action is in every detail contrived to test and reveal, with a surprising reversal, the moral quality of all three protagonists.

The short story, however, is a story that is *short;* that is, it differs from the novel in the dimension which Aristotle calls "magnitude," and this limitation in length imposes necessary differences both in the effects that can be achieved and in the choice and management of the elements to achieve those effects. Edgar Allan Poe, who is sometimes called the originator of the short story, was at any rate its first philosopher. What he calls "the prose tale" is a narrative that can be read at one sitting of from one-half hour to two hours, and is limited to "a certain unique or single effect," to which every detail is subordinate. (Review of Hawthorne's *Twice-Told Tales*, 1842.) Poe's comment applies to many short stories, and it points to the economy of management which the shortness of the form always imposes in some degree. The short story writer, compared to the novelist, introduces a limited number of characters, and cannot afford the space for leisurely character analysis and evolution. He usually begins the story close to, or even at, the climax, minimizes both exposition and the details of setting, keeps the complication down, often, to a single episode, and clears up the denouement quickly—sometimes in a sentence or two. There are many good short stories that depart from this paradigm in various ways, and it must be remembered that the term covers a great variety of prose narratives, all the way from the **short short story,** which is a slightly elaborated anecdote, to such complex and extended forms as Joseph Conrad's "Heart of Darkness" and Katherine Anne Porter's "Pale Horse, Pale Rider," which are sometimes called **novelettes.**

Historically, the short narrative, in verse or prose, is one of the oldest and most widespread of literary forms. For some early types which approximate the short story, see **fable, parable,** and **exemplum** (under **Allegory**), **Ballad,** and **novella** and **picaresque story** (under **Novel**). Another early form is the **folk tale,** or, in the German term, **Märchen,** a prose story which, like the folk ballad, was anonymous and passed on by oral tradition. These tales often deal with legendary matters, or with magic and enchantment; many of the fairy stories now published for children were originally folk tales. The Breton **lai** was a verse narrative, composed by courtly poets of about the twelfth century, and supposed to be based on Celtic legends. The **fabliau** was another medieval form that flourished in the twelfth century and later. It was a short comic tale in verse that dealt with middle-class or lower-class characters, realistically, satirically, and with a gay delight in the ribald. Chaucer, who wrote one of the best of serious stories in verse, the exemplum of Death and the Rioters in "The Pardoner's Tale," also wrote one of the best of fabliaux, the hilarious "Miller's Tale." Tales continued to be written in every century, but the prose short story in its recognizably modern form was developed by such writers as Washington Irving, Hawthorne, and Poe in America, Sir Walter Scott in England, and E. T. A. Hoffman in Germany. The short story, as the staple of "pulp," "slick," and "quality" magazines alike, is now the most widely read of literary forms. Refer to

Henry S. Canby, *The Short Story in English* (1909), and Seán O'Faoláin, *The Short Story* (1948).

Simile. See **Figurative language.**

Slapstick. See **Comedy.**

Soliloquy. See **Convention and Tradition** and **Dramatic monologue.**

Sonnet is the name for a lyric stanza form consisting of fourteen lines and written in an elaborate rhyme scheme which, in English, usually follows one of two patterns. The **Petrarchan sonnet,** named after the Italian writer, Petrarch (1304–1374), is divided into **octave** (8 lines) and **sestet** (6 lines) by the rhyme scheme: *a b b a a b b a   c d e c d e.* The sestet is variable, sometimes containing only two instead of three rhymes, and with the rhymes in differing arrangements. Petrarch's sonnets were first imitated in England by Sir Thomas Wyatt in the early sixteenth century (see **Conceit**); the form was later used by Milton, Wordsworth, D. G. Rossetti, and other sonneteers. English experimenters in the sixteenth century also developed a new form of the sonnet, called the **English** or **Shakespearean sonnet,** in which the rhyme scheme falls into three quatrains (4-line units) and a concluding couplet: *a b a b   c d c d   e f e f   g g.*

The sonnet has been a popular form because it is just long enough to permit a fairly complex lyric development, yet so short, and so exigent in its rhymes, as to pose a standing challenge to the artistry of the poet. The rhyme pattern of the Petrarchan sonnet has on the whole favored a statement of problem, situation, or incident in the octave, with a resolution in the sestet. The English form sometimes falls into a similar division of material, and sometimes presents a repetition-with-variation of the statement in the three quatrains; the final couplet, however, usually imposes an epigrammatic turn at the end. In Drayton's fine English sonnet, "Since there's no help, come let us kiss and part," the lover brusquely declares in the first two quatrains that he is glad the affair is cleanly broken off, pauses in the third quatrain as though at the threshold, and in the last two rhymed lines suddenly drops his swagger to make one last plea. Here are the concluding quatrain and couplet:

> Now at the last gasp of love's latest breath,
> When, his pulse failing, passion speechless lies,
> When faith is kneeling by his bed of death,
> And innocence is closing up his eyes,
>> Now if thou wouldst, when all have given him over,
>> From death to life thou mightst him yet recover.

A number of sixteenth-century English poets, including Sidney, Spenser, and Shakespeare, followed Petrarch's example and wrote a **sonnet sequence,** in which a series of sonnets are linked together by exploring various aspects of a relationship between lovers, or by indicating a development in that relationship which constitutes a kind of implicit plot. D. G. Rossetti's *House of Life,* Elizabeth Barrett Browning's *Sonnets from the Portuguese,* and William Ellery Leonard's *Two Lives* are later examples of the sonnet sequence. Refer to L. C. John, *The Elizabethan Sonnet Sequences* (1938). See also **Lyric, Rhyme,** and **Stanza.**

Spenserian stanza. See **Stanza.**

Spondee. See **Meter.**

Sprung rhythm. See **Meter.**

Stanza. A stanza is a division in the formal pattern of a poem. Usually the stanzas of a given poem are uniform in the number and length of the component lines and in the rhyme scheme. Some poems, however, are composed of variable stanzas (see, e.g., **irregular ode** under **Ode**), and some unrhymed poems are divided into stanzaic sections. Of the great variety of English stanza forms, many have no special names but must be described by specifying the number of lines, the kind and number of feet in each line, and the pattern of the rhyming words (see **Meter** and **Rhyme**). Some stanzas, however, have been used so repeatedly that they have been given the convenience of a name, as follows:

The **couplet** is a pair of rhymed lines (see **Couplet**). The **tercet** is a three-line stanza, usually with a single rhyme, in which the lines may be of the same or of different lengths. Robert Herrick's "Upon Julia's Clothes" is written in tercets of iambic tetrameter, but in Richard Crashaw's "Wishes to His Supposed Mistress," the lines of each tercet are, successively, in dimeter, trimeter, and tetrameter:

> Who e'er she be
> That not impossible she
> That shall command my heart and me.

The Italian form, **terza rima,** is composed of tercets which are not separate stanzas, because each is joined to the one preceding and the one following by a common rhyme: *a b a,   b c b,   c d c,   d e d,* and so on. Dante composed his *Divine Comedy* in terza rima; but although Sir Thomas Wyatt introduced the form early in the sixteenth century, it has never been widely used in English, in which rhymes are harder to find than in Italian. Shelley, however, used a modified version of terza rima in his "Ode to the West Wind," and Browning adopted it in "The Statue and the Bust."

The **quatrain,** or four-line stanza, is the most common in English poetry, and is employed with various meters and rhyme schemes. The **ballad stanza** (see under **Ballad**) is one common quatrain, and the **heroic quatrain,** in five-stress iambic verses rhyming *a b a b*, is the stanza of Gray's "Elegy Written in a Country Churchyard." The four-stress iambic quatrain rhyming *a b b a* is often called the "In Memoriam stanza," from its use in Tennyson's long elegy.

Chaucer introduced a seven-line, iambic pentameter stanza rhyming *a b a b b c c*, called **rime royal,** which he used for continuous narrative in *Troilus and Criseyde* and other poems. Like terza rima and the sonnet, **ottava rima** was brought from Italian into English poetry by Sir Thomas Wyatt. As the name indicates, this stanza has eight lines, rhyming *a b a b a b c c*. It has been employed by a number of English poets, but it is peculiarly the stanza which enabled Byron to discover what he was born to write, the great comic poem *Don Juan:*

> Juan was taught from out the best edition,
> Expurgated by learned men, who place,
> Judiciously, from out the schoolboy's vision,
> The grosser parts; but, fearful to deface
> Too much their modest bard by this omission,
> And pitying sore this mutilated case,
> They only add them all in an appendix,
> Which saves, in fact, the trouble of an index.

A still longer stanza is the **Spenserian,** devised by Edmund Spenser for *The Faerie Queene*—nine lines, the first eight iambic pentameter and the last iambic hexameter, or an **Alexandrine** (see **Meter**). The rhyme scheme is *a b a b b c b c c*. Enchanted by Spenser's music, many other poets have attempted the form in spite of its difficulties. Its greatest successes have been in poems which, like *The Faerie Queene*, move leisurely, with ample time for unrolling the richly textured stanzas: James Thomson's "The Castle of Indolence," Keats's "Eve of St. Agnes," Shelley's "Adonais," and the narrative part of Tennyson's "The Lotus Eaters."

A component in some stanzas is the **refrain,** which consists of one or more lines repeated, sometimes with slight changes, and usually at the end of each stanza in a poem. It is found in many ballads, and is a frequent element in the Elizabethan lyric, sometimes in a nonsense form: "With a hey, and a ho, and a hey nonino." A famous refrain occurs at the end of each stanza of Spenser's "Epithalamion": "The woods shall to me answer, and my echo ring."

There are also a number of elaborate stanza forms imported from France—the **rondeau,** the **villanelle,** the **triolet**—whose intricate patterns of rhyme and line repetitions are used mainly for light verse (see **Vers de société**). These forms were exploited by Andrew Lang and Austin Dobson in the Victorian period; their recent use by W. H. Auden,

William Empson, and others is a sign of the renewed interest in metrical artifice. These stanzas, like the others listed here, are conveniently classified, discussed, and exemplified in R. M. Alden, *English Verse* (1903); see also **Blank verse** and **Sonnet**.

Stock characters are character types which recur repeatedly in a particular literary genre, and so are recognizable as a convention of the form (see **Convention and Tradition**). Elizabethan romantic comedy almost invariably had a heroine disguised as a handsome young man, and the Elizabethan comedy of intrigue usually incorporated the clever servant who connives with his master to fleece another stock character, the stupid "gull" (see **Comedy**). Nineteenth-century comedy exploited the stock Englishman with a monocle, an exaggerated Oxford accent, and a defective sense of humor; and we still recognize, in both comedy and vaudeville, the stage Englishman, Irishman, Scotsman, Negro, and so on. Western stories developed the tight-lipped sheriff who lets his gun do the talking for him, while a familiar figure in modern fiction is the stoical Hemingway hero, unillusioned but faithful to his primal code of honor and loyalty in a civilization grown effete and corrupt. The evaluation of a literary character does not depend simply on whether an author adopts a stock type, but on how well he re-creates and individualizes it. Two of Shakespeare's greatest characters are recognizably conventional: Falstaff is a version of the familiar braggart soldier, or *miles gloriosus*, and Hamlet combines the attributes of the hero of revenge tragedy (see under **Tragedy**) with those of the Elizabethan melancholic man.

Stock situations are the counterparts in plot of stock characters; that is, they are often-used sequences of action. The Horatio Alger books are all variations on the rags-to-riches-by-pluck-and-luck plot, and we readily recognize the boy-meets-girl theme in moving pictures and popular fiction. Some modern critics distinguish certain stock characters and plot elements, such as the fatal woman and the journey to the underworld, as "archetypal patterns," which are held to recur, not by literary convention, but because they express universal aspects of man's unconscious mind (see **Archetype**).

A **stock response** is an habitual and stereotyped reaction to a literary work or passage, in contrast to a response that is flexibly and discriminatingly adapted to the work's distinctive qualities. See I. A. Richards, *Practical Criticism* (1930), Chap. 5, and compare **Cliché**.

Stream of consciousness. See **Novel**.

Stress. See **Meter**.

Strophe. See **Ode**.

Structure and texture. Most modern critics agree in the use of the term "structure" for the organization, or over-all design, or "form" of a particular literary work, to which, if the work is a good one, the component parts are regarded as being contributive but subordinate. (See, for example, the many kinds of "structures" mentioned in the articles on **Allegory, Comedy, Didactic, Lyric, Novel, Plot and Character, Tragedy.**) But critics disagree widely on the principles, or basic concepts, which they use in determining what is the key to literary structure; they disagree also on whether there is one universal structure found in all good poems, or whether there is a typical structure for each genre, or whether each literary work has a structure uniquely its own. (See **Genre** and **Criticism.**) The range and causes of these disagreements have been analyzed by R. S. Crane, *The Languages of Criticism and the Structure of Poetry* (1953).

John Crowe Ransom has been rather widely echoed in his analysis of a poem into the two elements of "logical structure," or paraphrasable argument, and "local texture," the added particularities of image and detail which, in Ransom's analysis, make it a poem rather than a piece of expository prose. See, e.g., Ransom's *The New Criticism* (1941), pp. 268–275, and his "Criticism as Pure Speculation," in *The Intent of the Critic,* ed. D. A. Stauffer (1941). In many critical uses, however, "texture" refers merely to the sensuous qualities of the verbal surface of a work, or to the density and pattern of the imagery. See **Abstract and Concrete** and **Imagery.**

Style is a characteristic manner of expression in prose or verse—it is *how* a speaker or writer says whatever he says. The style of a work may be analyzed in terms of its diction, or choice of words (see **Diction**); the frequency and types of its figures of speech (see **Figurative language**); its rhythmic patterns; the structure of its sentences; and its rhetorical devices and effects (see **Rhetorical figures**). Two types of sentence structure are often distinguished in analyzing prose style. The **periodic sentence** is one in which the parts, or "members," are so composed that the sense remains suspended until the close; the effect tends to be formal and oratorical. In the **nonperiodic,** or **loose, sentence,** more relaxed and conversational in effect, the members are joined in a continuous and running fashion, so that the sentence could have been concluded by inserting a period at one or more places before the actual close.

Styles are often classified according to a literary period or tradition ("Restoration prose style," "the metaphysical style"); according to an influential work ("Biblical style," "Euphuism"—see **Euphuism**); according to subject matter or use ("scientific" vs. "poetic" style, "journalese"); or according to the distinctive practice of an individual author (the "Shakespearean" or "Miltonic" or "Johnsonian" style). Styles at one time were also classified into various levels—e.g., high (or grand), middle, and low (or plain)—and the doctrine of **decorum,** or propriety, demanded that the level of style be appropriate to the speaker, the occasion, and the literary genre. (See **Epic, Genre,** and **Neoclassic and Romantic.**) Although the strict doctrine of decorum has lapsed, modern speakers and prose writers still adapt the technicality and formality of their style to their subject matter and to the audience to which they address themselves (see **Tone**). And most modern poets still make a distinction between the levels of style they use in, let us say, a serious and a satirical poem; see, e.g., the difference in style between the lyrics and *Cantos* of Ezra Pound.

Refer to John Middleton Murry, *The Problem of Style* (1925); Bonamy Dobree, *Modern Prose Style* (1934); and Paull Baum, *The Other Harmony of Prose* (1952).

Subjective. See **Objective and Subjective.**

Suspense and **Surprise.** See **Plot and Character.**

Symbol. A symbol, in the broadest use of the term, is anything which signifies something else; in this sense, all words are symbols. As commonly used in criticism, however, "symbol" is applied only to a word or phrase signifying an object which itself has significance; that is, the object referred to has a range of meaning beyond itself. Some symbols are "conventional," or "public"; thus "the Cross," "the Red, White, and Blue," "the Good Shepherd" are terms that signify objects of which the symbolic meanings are widely known. Poets, like all of us, use these conventional symbols; but some poets also use "private symbols," which are not widely known, or which they develop for themselves (usually by expanding and elaborating pre-existing associations of an object), and these set a more difficult problem in interpretation.

Take as an example the word "rose," which in its literal meaning is a kind of flower. In Burns's line, "O my love's like a red, red rose," the word is used as a simile, and in the version "O my love is a red, red rose," it is used as a metaphor. William Blake wrote:

> O Rose, thou art sick!
> The invisible worm
> That flies in the night,
> In the howling storm,
>
> Has found out thy bed
> Of crimson joy,
> And his dark secret love
> Does thy life destroy.

This rose is not the vehicle for a simile or a metaphor, because it lacks the paired subject—"my love," in the examples just cited—which is char acteristic of these figures (see under **Figurative language**). Blake's rose *is* a rose—yet it is also something more; words like "bed," "joy," "love," indicate that the described object has a further range of significance which makes it a symbol. But Blake's rose is not, like the symbolic rose of Dante's *Paradiso* and other medieval poems, an element in a complex set of traditional religious symbols which were widely known to contemporary readers. Only from the clues in Blake's poem itself, supplemented by a knowledge of parallel elements in his other poems, do we come to see that Blake's worm-eaten rose symbolizes such matters as the destruction wrought by furtiveness, deceit, and hypocrisy in what should be a frank and joyous relationship of physical love.

Other romantic poets, particularly Shelley, employed a number of symbols in their poetry, but Blake's persistent and sustained symbolic mode of writing had no close parallel until the Symbolist movement of the followers of the French poet, Baudelaire, during the later nineteenth century. The period since the first World War has been a notable era of **symbolism** in literature. Many important writers of this period use symbol systems in part drawn from largely forgotten religious and esoteric traditions and in part developed by themselves. Some of the most notable works of the age are symbolic in every element: in their settings, their agents, their actions, and their language. Instances of a persistently symbolist procedure can be found in short lyrics (Yeats's "Byzantium" poems), longer poems (Eliot's "The Waste Land"), dramas (Elmer Rice's *The Adding Machine*), and novels (Kafka's *The Trial*, Joyce's *Ulysses*). See **Expressionism,** and refer to Edmund Wilson, *Axel's Castle* (1936).

Sympathy. See **Empathy and Sympathy.**

Synecdoche. See **Figurative language.**

Synesthesia is the experience of two or more modes of sensation when only one sense is being stimulated. In literature the term is applied to passages in which one kind of sensation is described in terms of another; for example, color is attributed to sounds, odor to colors, sound to odors, and so on. A complex example of this phenomenon, sometimes also called "sense transference" or "sense analogy," is this passage from Shelley's "The Sensitive Plant":

> And the hyacinth purple, and white, and blue,
> Which flung from its bells a sweet peal anew
> Of music so delicate, soft, and intense,
> It was felt like an odor within the sense.

The colored flowers send out a peal of music which affects the sense as though it were (what it in fact originally was) the scent of the hyacinths. Keats, in the "Ode to a Nightingale," calls for a draught of cool wine

Tasting of Flora and the country *green,*
Dance, and Provençal *song,* and *sunburnt* mirth;

tasting, that is, of sight, color, motion, sound, and heat. This type of imagery was assiduously exploited by the French Symbolists of the latter nineteenth century; see Baudelaire's sonnet, *"Correspondances,"* and Rimbaud's sonnet on the color of vowel sounds: "A black, E white, I red, U green, O blue." Consult June Downey, *Creative Imagination* (1929).

Tenor and vehicle. See **metaphor** under **Figurative language.**

Tension. The word "tension" has frequently been used in criticism since Allen Tate proposed it as a term to be made by "lopping the prefixes off the logical terms *ex*tension and *in*tension." In logic the "intension" of a word is the abstract set of attributes which must be possessed by the objects to which the word can be applied, and the "extension" of a word is the specific object or set of objects to which it applies. The meaning of good poetry, according to Tate, "is its 'tension,' the full organized body of all the extension and intension that we can find in it" ("Tension in Poetry," 1938). By this statement, it would seem, he means that a good poem includes both abstract and concrete meaning in an integral rela- tion—the universal in the particular, the idea in the image (see **Abstract and Concrete**). Other critics use "tension" to describe poetry which exhibits an equilibrium of seriousness and irony, or "a pattern of resolved stresses," or any other mode of that stability-in-conflict which is the favorite way in modern criticism of conceiving the organization of a poem (see **Criticism**). And some critics, perhaps in doubt about the philosophy behind Tate's use of the term, simply apply "tension" to any poem in which the parts seem tightly rather than loosely put together.

Tercet. See **Stanza.**

Terza rima. See **Stanza.**

Texture. See **Structure and Texture.**

Theme. See **Motif.**

Threnody. See **Elegy.**

Tone. In recent criticism "tone" is often employed, after the example of I. A. Richards, for the attitudes to the subject matter and to the audience implied in a discourse or literary piece. The tone of a passage might be characterized, for example, as formal or intimate, solemn or playful, serious or ironic, condescending or obsequious. Compare **Irony** and **Style,** and refer to I. A. Richards, *Practical Criticism* (1929), Part III, Chaps. 1 and 3.

Tradition. See **Convention and Tradition.**

Tragedy. The term "tragedy" is broadly applied to literary, and especially to dramatic, representations of serious actions which turn out disastrously for the chief character (compare **Comedy**). Discussions of tragedy almost always begin—although they should not end—with Aristotle's classic analysis in the *Poetics.* Aristotle based his discussion on the tragedies of the Greek dramatists such as Aeschylus, Sophocles, and Euripides. In the intervening two thousand years and more, many new types of serious plots with unhappy endings have been developed which Aristotle, whose method was that of induction from existing dramas, could not foresee. Aristotle's theory of tragedy has been misused in two main ways. Sometimes it is stretched so that it is made to apply to all modern forms of tragedy, with the result both of blurring Aristotle's categories and flattening out the distinctive differences between diverse kinds of tragedy. And sometimes Aristotle's theory, rigidly interpreted as constituting the unique formula for all tragedy, is used to condemn as debased or hybrid forms many post-Aristotelian works which are eminent artistic successes, though each after its own fashion. When flexibly managed, however, Aristotle's concepts continue to be applicable, at least in part, to many types of serious plots; and they are always a convenient and suggestive starting point for establishing the differentiae of the non-Aristotelian forms of tragic construction.

Aristotle defined tragedy as "the imitation of an action that is serious and also, as having magnitude, complete in itself," in the medium of poetic language, and in the manner of dramatic rather than narrative presentation, "with incidents arousing pity and fear, wherewith to accomplish its catharsis of such emotions." Precisely how to interpret Aristotle's **catharsis,** or "purgation" of pity and fear, has been much disputed, but two things seem clear. Aristotle in the first place points to the undeniable, if extraordinary, fact that many tragic representations of suffering and defeat leave an audience feeling, not depressed, but relieved and almost elated. And in the second place, Aristotle uses this distinctive effect of the "tragic pleasure of pity and fear" as the basic way to distinguish tragic from comic and other forms, and as the aim which above all determines the selection, treatment, and ordering of the component parts of a tragedy.

For example, Aristotle says that the tragic hero will most effectively arouse pity and fear if he is neither thoroughly good nor thoroughly evil, but a man like any of us, though the tragic effect will be stronger if he is rather better than most of us. Such a man is exhibited as suffering a change in fortune from happiness to misery because of a mistaken act due to his **hamartia**—that is, his "tragic flaw" or "tragic error in judgment." (One form of hamartia especially appealing to the Greek tragic poets was **hubris,** that pride or overconfidence which leads a man to overlook a divine warning, or to break a moral law.) The tragic hero accordingly moves us to pity, because the misfortune is greater than he has deserved, and to fear, because we recognize similar possibilities and consequences in our own fallible selves. Aristotle also grounds his analysis of "the very structure and incidents of the play"—that is, the plot—on the same principle, the aim of evoking "tragic fear and pity"; for the type of plot which produces the most effective catharsis is that in which events move from a beginning, through complication, to a catastrophe, or tragic reversal, of the hero's fortune. (See **Plot and Character.**)

The Middle Ages, lacking direct knowledge either of classical tragedies or Aristotle's theory, conceived tragedy to be simply the story of an eminent person who, deservedly or undeservedly, is brought from prosperity to wretchedness by an unpredictable turn of fortune's wheel. The short anecdotes in Chaucer's "Monk's Tale" are all "tragedies" of this kind. With the Elizabethan era came both the beginning and the acme of dramatic tragedy in England. The tragedies of the period between 1585 and 1625 owed a good deal to the native religious drama of the Middle Ages (see **Miracle and Morality plays**), but a most important contribution came from the plays of the Roman writer, Seneca. **Senecan tragedy** provided the model for a fully developed five-act drama with a formal rhetorical style of dialogue; and it produced, in the Elizabethan age, two main lines of development. One of these consisted of the rather academic tragedies, constructed according to the "rules" of the unities and decorum, and usually including a classic "chorus." (See **chorus, rules** under **Neoclassic and Romantic,** and **unities** under **Plot and Character.**) The other development was the **revenge tragedy,** or **tragedy of blood,** deriving from Seneca's favorite subjects of revenge, adultery, incest, murder, mutilation, and general carnage. Thomas Kyd's *Spanish Tragedy* (1586) established this popular Elizabethan form, based on a quest for revenge, and including a ghost, insanity, suicide, a play-within-a-play, sensational incidents, and a bloody ending. Marlowe's *The Jew of Malta* and Shakespeare's *Titus Andronicus* also belong in this convention, which had its apotheosis in Shakespeare's *Hamlet.*

Many of the best Elizabethan tragedies by Marlowe, Shakespeare, Heywood, Chapman, Middleton, Webster, Beaumont and Fletcher, and Massinger deviate radically from the Aristotelian form. Shakespeare's *Othello* is entirely amenable to Aristotelian categories; but the hero of *Macbeth,* for example, is not a good man with a tragic flaw but a man who turns great gifts to evil purposes, and therefore, although he always retains a modicum of our admiration and sympathy, thoroughly deserves his destruction at the hands of his more admirable antagonists. Another departure from Aristotle's paradigm was the almost universal employment of humorous speeches and incidents, called **comic relief,** in the course of the serious action. Sometimes these were merely intrusive bits of comic dialogue and horseplay, but in other instances they were woven into the drama in such a way that they widened and enriched, rather than weakened, the tragic significance: examples are the gravediggers in *Hamlet,* the drunken porter in *Macbeth,* and the speeches of the Fool in *Lear.* A non-Aristotelian form which produced artistic masterpieces was the **tragicomedy.** This is a play in which the action is basically serious and seems to threaten disaster to the protagonist, but which eventuates in a happy reversal. The term "tragicomedy" is also applied to plays in which serious and comic elements are combined throughout the action, either in the mode of a double plot or of alternating episodes of gravity and humor. Examples of tragicomedy are Shakespeare's *Merchant of Venice* and *The Winter's Tale,* and Beaumont and Fletcher's *Philaster.*

The **heroic drama** was a form specific to the Restoration period. As Dryden defined it: "An heroic play ought to be an imitation, in little, of an heroic poem; and consequently . . . love and valour ought to be the subject of it." By "heroic poem" he meant epic, and the play attempted to imitate the epic by including a warrior-hero, an action involving the fate of an empire, and an elevated style, usually cast in the form of heroic couplets (see **Epic** and **Couplet**). A noble hero and heroine are typically represented in a situation in which their passionate love conflicts with the demands of honor and patriotic duty. Usually the central dilemma is obviously contrived, and the characters statuesque and unconvincing, while the attempt at a grand style tends to swell into bombast (see **Bombast**). Dryden's *Conquest of Granada* is one of the better heroic tragedies, but his greatest achievement in this mode was his heroic adaptation of Shakespeare's *Antony and Cleopatra,* which he called *All for Love.*

With few exceptions tragedy, until the end of the seventeenth century, was written mainly in verse and had as protagonists men of high political and military rank whose fate affected to some degree the fortunes of a state. A few Elizabethan tragedies dealt with lower-class characters, but it remained for eighteenth-century writers to popularize the **bourgeois,** or **domestic, tragedy,** written in prose and presenting a protagonist from the common ranks in a commonplace disaster. George Lillo's *George Barnwell, or the London Merchant,* written in 1731, is still read, at least in college courses; since that time, most tragedies have been concerned with middle-class, or even working-class, heroes and heroines. The nineteenth century in England produced few notable tragedies but many

melodramas. *Melos* is Greek for song, and the term refers to the music frequently used to fortify the emotional tone of the various scenes. Melodrama is sometimes said to bear the same relation to tragedy that farce does to comedy (see under **Comedy**). The protagonists are pure as the driven snow and the antagonists luridly evil, while credibility of both character and action is sacrificed for violent effect, in a drama contrived according to an emotional opportunism. Melodramas such as *Sweeney Todd, The Demon Barber of Fleet Street* (1842) and *Ten Nights in a Bar-room* (1858) are still sometimes produced, but alas! no longer for thrills but for laughs. A melodrama usually ended, not with a catastrophe, but with an exact demonstration of **poetic justice,** in which earthly rewards and punishments are distributed in proportion to the deserts of the characters.

The great Norwegian dramatist, Henrik Ibsen, who did more than anyone to revive tragedy in the latter nineteenth century, popularized the **problem play,** or **drama of ideas.** In this dramatic type (which sometimes has a comic instead of a tragic ending) the situation of the protagonist is clearly rendered to show that it is only an instance of a general social problem. This problem may be one of the inadequate scope allowed to a woman in a middle-class nineteenth-century family (Ibsen's *A Doll's House*); or of the morality of prostitution as a phenomenon in a capitalist society (Shaw's *Mrs. Warren's Profession*); or of the waste yet seeming inevitability of conflict between management and workers in an industrial concern (Galsworthy's *Strife*). The dramatist often manages the plot in such a way as to indicate that he favors a solution of the problem which is at odds with prevailing opinion; many problem plays therefore are, strictly speaking, didactic forms of drama (see **Didactic**).

Tragedy since the first World War has in many cases been radically experimental, sometimes in a modern variation upon an archaic form, as in T. S. Eliot's poetic morality play, *Murder in the Cathedral,* and sometimes in new directions. A number of tragedies by writers such as Synge, O'Casey, Eugene O'Neill, and more recently Tennessee Williams and Arthur Miller, show the double influence of the once opposed literary movements known as Symbolism and Naturalism (see **Realism and Naturalism** and **Symbol**). Useful references are A. C. Bradley, *Shakespearean Tragedy* (1904); F. L. Lucas, *Tragedy in Relation to Aristotle's Poetics* (1927); John Gassner, *Masters of the Drama* (1940).

Travesty. See **Burlesque and Parody.**

Triolet. See **Stanza.**

Trochee. See **Meter.**

Trope. See **Figurative language.**

Understatement. See **Irony.**

Unities, Dramatic. See **Plot and Character.**

Vers de société, or "society verse," is brief epigrammatic or lyrical verse dealing with the surface concerns or events of polite society. (See **Epigram** and **Lyric.**) It is sometimes satiric, but in the mood of badinage rather than severity; and when it deals with love, it does so flirtatiously or in the mode of elegant and witty compliment, rather than with high seriousness. The tone is conversational, the style deft, and the form polished and at times very elaborate; most poems using the intricate French stanzas of the vilanelle, triolet, and rondeau are society verse (see under **Stanza**). **Light verse** is the larger genre of which society verse is a species; it deals in the same light-hearted but sometimes mordant fashion with all aspects of the human comedy. Among the artificers of light and society verse are the Cavalier poets (see **Caroline Period**), Matthew Prior, Alexander Pope, Austin Dobson, Frederick Locker-Lampson, and the modern writers W. H. Auden, Morris Bishop, and Phyllis McGinley. The limerick is the form of light verse everyone knows, and most of us have practiced. See W. H. Auden, ed., *The Oxford Book of Light Verse* (1938).

Verse. See **Meter.** For **verse paragraph,** see **Blank verse.**

Victorian Period. The beginning of the Victorian Period is dated sometimes as 1832 (the passage of the first Reform Bill) and sometimes as 1837 (the accession of Queen Victoria); it extends to the death of Victoria in 1901. (See **Romantic Period.**) Much writing of the period, whether didactic or imaginative, in prose or in verse, reflected current social, economic, and intellectual problems—e.g., the industrial revolution and its effects on the physical scene and the economic structure of England, the pressures toward political and social reform, and the impact on philosophy and religious orthodoxy of the theory of evolution. It was an age of immense literary activity. The most prominent poets were Tennyson, Browning, and Arnold; the most prominent essayists were Carlyle, Ruskin, and Arnold; the most prominent of many excellent novelists were Dickens, Thackeray, George Eliot, Meredith, Trollope, Hardy, and Samuel Butler.

Vilanelle. See **Stanza.**

Wit and Humor. The word "wit" once meant "intelligence" or "knowledge," a sense it still keeps in terms like "half-wit" and "unwittingly." In the seventeenth century "wit" was often applied, in criticism, to the characteristic use of paradox and surprising combinations of ideas in the writings of metaphysical poets (see **Metaphysical poets**), and in the eighteenth century there were various attempts to distinguish between the "false wit" of Cowley and other metaphysical writers and the "true wit" recommended for the expression of thought in neoclassic poetry (see **Neoclassic and Romantic**). The term has now become still more specialized. "Wit," in common usage, is applied to a brief and deftly phrased expression, intentionally contrived to produce a shock of comic surprise. The surprise is usually the result of an unexpected, but plausible, connection or distinction between ideas, or of the sudden frustration of expectation. Philip Guedalla said, "History repeats itself: historians repeat each other." The trite comment about history turns out to be comically appropriate, with an unlooked for turn of meaning, to the writers of history as well. "The only sure way to double your money," Abe Martin remarked, "is to fold it and put it in your hip pocket." The eagerly awaited advice is tendered us, but in a way which is startlingly literal and practical. The resulting laughter, in the phrase of Immanuel Kant, arises "from the sudden transformation of a strained expectation into nothing"; or perhaps it would be more accurate to say, from the sudden satisfaction of an expectation in a way we did not expect. Abe Martin's remark is what Freud called "harmless wit," evoking a laugh or smile without malice. "Tendency wit," on the other hand, is derisive, directing the laugh at a particular object, or butt. "Mr. James Payn," Oscar Wilde commented on a contemporary novelist, "hunts down the obvious with the enthusiasm of a short-sighted detective. As one turns over the pages, the suspense of the author becomes almost unbearable." Wit often approximates the form of an epigram (see **Epigram**) and utilizes a number of devices defined elsewhere, such as **Irony** and (under **Figurative language**) **pun** and **paradox**.

Repartee is a term aptly borrowed from fencing to signify a contest of wit between two or more people, in which each tries to cap the remark of the other, or to turn it to his own purpose. The Earl of Rochester suggested as an appropriate epitaph for Charles II:

> Here lies our sovereign lord the King,
> Whose word no man relies on;
> He never says a foolish thing,
> And never does a wise one.

Although amused by the epigram, King Charles said that the paradox was easily explained: he did his own talking, but all his actions were dictated by his ministers. In King Charles's own period, stage comedies usually included long episodes of sustained repartee. The classic example is the discussion of the marriage contract in Congreve's *The Way of the World,* Act IV (see **Restoration comedy** under **Comedy**).

Humor, through the Renaissance period, was a physiological term for the four primary fluids of the human body: blood, phlegm, choler (or yellow bile), and melancholy (or black bile). The "temperament," or mixture, of these humors was thought to determine both a man's physical condition and his character. A preponderance of one or another humor in a temperament was supposed to produce four types of disposition, whose names have survived the underlying theory: sanguine (from *sanguis,* blood), phlegmatic, choleric, and melancholic. Ben Jonson based on this physiology his theory of the **comedy of humors,** in which each person is regarded as motivated by a preponderant humor that gives him a characteristic bias or eccentricity of disposition. See Ben Jonson's "Induction" to his *Every Man in his Humour* (1598).

The present meaning of the word "humor" has developed from the comic attributes of this "humorous" character in the Elizabethan period. Humor, like wit, can be predicated of a comic speech, but in that case it differs from wit in one or both of two ways. Wit, as we saw, is always intentionally comic, while humor may be unintentional; and a humorous saying is not cast in the neat and startling epigrammatic form of wit. For example, the discussion of the mode of life of the goldfish in Central Park by the irascible taxi driver in J. D. Salinger's *The Catcher in the Rye* is unintentionally but superbly humorous, while the speech of Mr. Bennet in Austen's *Pride and Prejudice,* or of Mercutio in *Romeo and Juliet,* is intentionally humorous, though rarely expressed in the rhetorical shape of wit. Still more important is the difference that wit is always verbal, while humor applies to what is laughable in a person's appearance and his actions, as well as in what he says. For example, we find humor in the wordless pantomime of Charlie Chaplin and in the sometimes uncaptioned cartoons in the *New Yorker.* In a thoroughly humorous situation, the sources of the fun are more complex. In Act III, scene IV, of *Twelfth Night,* Malvolio's appearance and actions, and his speech as well, are humorous, but all despite his own intentions. One source of the greatness in a comic creation like Shakespeare's Falstaff is that he exhibits every possible kind of comedy. Falstaff is humorous in the way he looks and in what he does; what he says is always either witty or humorous; while his actions and speech are sometimes humorous against his intention, and often humorous even beyond his intention.

It will be apparent by now that humor is a species of the **comic.** We may extend the distinction Freud made between harmless and tendency wit and say that humor is pure or "harmless" comedy, in which we are made to laugh because a person is ridiculous but not because he is being ridiculed. When we are made to laugh with a touch of contempt or malice, the situation is an instance, not of the humorously comic, but of "tendency" comedy, in which the laughter is derisive and is being used as a weapon. Tendency comedy, together with tendency wit, are the techniques that the satirist employs in his enterprise of diminishing and deriding his subjects. See **comic** under **Satire,** and refer to Max Eastman, *Enjoyment of Laughter* (1936).

Zeugma. See **Rhetorical figures.**